100
scientists
who made
history

Remarkable
scientists
who shaped
our world

DK London

Senior editor Shaila Brown
Senior art editor Jacqui Swan
Project editor Ben Ffrancon Davies
Jacket editor Claire Gell
Jacket designer Surabhi Wadhwa
Jacket design development manager
Sophia MTT
Producer, pre-production
Jacqueline Street
Producer Anna Vallarino

Managing editor Lisa Gillespie
Managing art editor Owen Peyton Jones
Publisher Andrew Macintyre
Associate publishing director
Liz Wheeler
Art director Karen Self
Design director Phil Ormerod
Publishing director Jonathan Metcalf

DK Delhi

Senior editor Sreshtha Bhattacharya
Project editor Priyanka Kharbanda
Project art editor Neha Sharma
Editorial team Isha Sharma, Vatsal Verma
Art editors Nidhi Rastogi, Sachin Singh
Assistant art editors Baibhav Parida,
Rohit Bharadwaj, Ankita Das
Jacket designer Suhita Dharamjit
Jacket editorial coordinator
Priyanka Sharma
Senior DTP designer Harish Aggarwal
DTP designers Pawan Kumar,
Nityanand Kumar, Mohammad Rizwan
Picture researcher Sakshi Saluja
Managing jackets editor Saloni Singh
Picture researcher manager Taiyaba Khatoon
Pre-production manager Balwant Singh
Production manager Pankaj Sharma
Managing editor Kingshuk Ghoshal
Managing art editor Govind Mittal

First published in Great Britain in 2018
by Dorling Kindersley Limited,
80 Strand, London WC2R 0RL

A Penguin Random House Company
10 9 8 7 6 5 4 3
007 – 306255 – February/2018

A CIP catalogue record for this book is available from
the British Library.

ISBN: 978–0–2413–0432–7

Printed in China

A WORLD OF IDEAS:
SEE ALL THERE IS TO KNOW

www.dk.com

100 scientists who made history

Remarkable scientists who shaped our world

Written by Andrea Mills
and Stella Caldwell

Consultant Philip Parker

Contents

perceptive pioneers

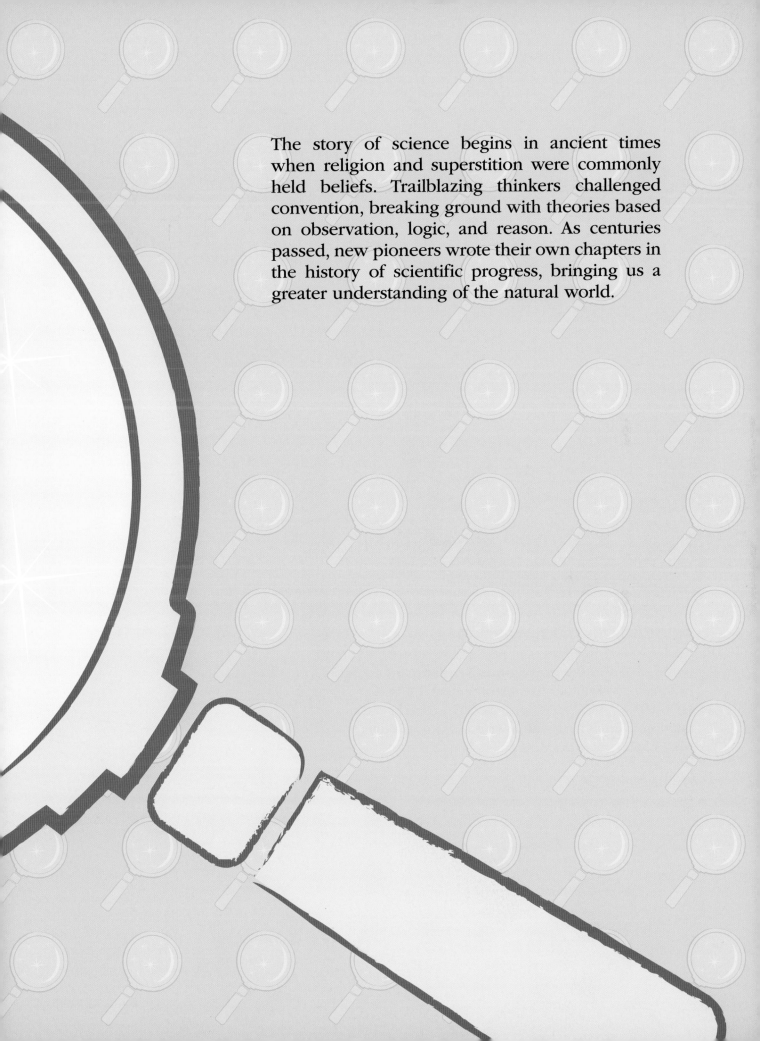

The story of science begins in ancient times when religion and superstition were commonly held beliefs. Trailblazing thinkers challenged convention, breaking ground with theories based on observation, logic, and reason. As centuries passed, new pioneers wrote their own chapters in the history of scientific progress, bringing us a greater understanding of the natural world.

Aristotle

The GREAT THINKER who dedicated his life to the pursuit of knowledge

The powerful ideas and writings of this famous natural philosopher survived the centuries.

Aristotle tutored Alexander in subjects such as biology, mathematics, and astronomy.

Foundations of knowledge

Born in Stagira, Greece, in 384 BCE, Aristotle enrolled at **Plato's prestigious Academy** in Athens as a teenager. He spent almost **TWO DECADES STUDYING** philosophy, science, and logic. Equipped with a wealth of knowledge, Aristotle travelled to Macedonia in 342 BCE and became a tutor. His student *Alexander the Great* later created the biggest empire ever seen.

Did you know?
Aristotle is believed to have had a stutter that caused him problems when speaking. Despite this, he tutored students throughout his life.

Aristotle was the first to recognize that whales and dolphins do not belong to the fish family.

Who came before...

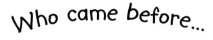

*Born in 624 BCE, **THALES OF MILETUS** is often called the world's first scientist. He believed that water was the original material of everything.*

*Philosopher **SOCRATES** was born in Athens, Greece, in 470 BCE. He believed that the way to achieve true wisdom was to question the things we think we know, favouring this method over standard lectures.*

Classifying nature

Fascinated with **biology and botany**, Aristotle was the first to classify nature by *defining different species, and dividing plants and animals into logical groups*. He drew animals in detail and studied their body parts and functions. While recording his observations, Aristotle founded the **SCIENCE OF ZOOLOGY** (the study of animals).

By the way...
I did make mistakes – I thought that planet Earth did not move, and that the human heart housed intelligence.

A medieval French translation of a page from Aristotle's book *Politics*.

Library of knowledge

Aristotle returned to Athens in 335 BCE, and established his own school, **THE LYCEUM**. He continued writing on every subject imaginable, from *poetry to politics*. He also **studied light**, and believed we can see objects because they emit light. By the time of his death in 322 BCE, he had written more than 200 books.

How he changed the world

Aristotle's use of observation, experimentation, and classification in scientific studies continues to influence and inspire the world more than 2,000 years later.

Who came after...

Scholar **ALHAZEN** made careful observations before testing his ideas. In the early 1000s, he proved that sight is the result of light from different objects hitting the eyes.

In 1735, Swedish botanist **CARL LINNAEUS** updated Aristotle's catalogue of classification by creating a modern, uniform system for naming and grouping organisms.

Greek greats

Many ancient Greek natural philosophers were gifted scientists who studied the world around them using reasoning and observation. A lot of their theories have stood the test of time and are still taught at schools today.

The Pythagorean theorem for right-angled triangles is $a^2 + b^2 = c^2$.

The first THINKERS who laid the foundations for future scientists

Pythagoras

Born on the Greek island of Samos in about 570 BCE, Pythagoras became a keen **MATHEMATICIAN**. He is best known for his *theorem of right-angled triangles*, which states that the square of the length of the hypotenuse (longest side of a triangle) is equal to the **sum of the squares of the lengths of the other two sides**.

Empedocles

In the 5th century BCE, poet and philosopher Empedocles proposed a theory that *every object* is a mixture of **FOUR ELEMENTS** of matter – **earth, air, fire, and water**. He thought that love and strife, or disagreement, filled the space between these elements, controlling and balancing them.

Fire

Water

Earth

Air

Democritus

Greek philosopher Democritus suggested **the existence of tiny particles of matter**. Around the 5th century BCE, he claimed all things must be made of very small pieces and called these **ATOMS**, making him a true pioneer of the theory that everything in the *Universe is made of atoms*. He was also the first to understand that the Milky Way is a distant galaxy.

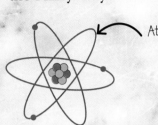

Atom

Did you know?
Democritus was known as the Laughing Philosopher because he was so cheerful.

Euclid

Geometry genius Euclid was the brains behind many theories about **shapes, space, and time**. He taught mathematics at Alexandria, the Egyptian city and centre of learning, before writing a collection of 13 geometry books called *The Elements* in around 300 BCE. Euclid's work was translated into many languages and formed the **FOUNDATIONS** of modern-day textbooks.

Euclid developed formulas for measuring circles and lines.

Hypatia

Hypatia was born in about 355 CE in Alexandria, Egypt, where she studied astronomy, mathematics, and philosophy. Her innovative ideas about **shapes drew huge audiences to her lectures**. She was also involved in developing the **PLANE ASTROLABE** – an instrument designed to *measure the position of the Sun and stars*.

Hypatia studied the curves created by different sections cut through cones.

Archimedes

A legendary life of EUREKA moments

This problem-solving mathematical genius, came up with calculations and clever inventions that have stayed afloat since ancient times.

EUREKA!

By the way...
Even though I'm known for mathematics and science, I also enjoyed poetry, art, and music.

Archimedes would have studied in the library of Alexandria – the greatest library of the ancient world.

Crown challenge

Born in about 287 BCE in Syracuse on the island of Sicily, Archimedes was taught in **Alexandria, Egypt**, at the school of Greek mathematician Euclid. He enjoyed using **MATHEMATICS** to solve problems and was given a challenge to work out if *King Hiero II's crown was made of pure gold*.

What came before...

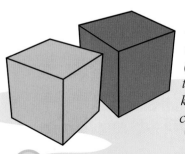

The world's **FIRST BOOK ABOUT GEOMETRY** *was developed by Hippocrates of Chios (470–410 BCE) – a merchant turned mathematician, known for his work with circles and cubes.*

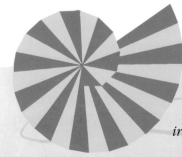

The **WHEEL OF THEODORUS**, *a spiral of consecutive right triangles, was constructed by mathematics wizard Theodorus of Cyrene (465–398 BCE). He also studied square roots and irrational numbers.*

Brainy bath time

The breakthrough came at bath time when Archimedes noticed overflowing water. He had **displaced** (moved aside) the same volume of water as the volume of his submerged body. Shouting "Eureka!" (I've found it!), Archimedes realized this was the **SOLUTION TO MEASURING VOLUME** – silver is lighter than gold, so a silver crown of equal weight would have a higher volume and displace more water. As a result, he proved *the king's crown was a combination of silver and gold*.

Colossal calculations

Archimedes worked on *many more theories*. He wanted to know **how many grains of sand would fill the Universe**. However, the Greek number system was based on letters, such as A=1, B=2, C=3, and there were not enough letters to represent large numbers, so Archimedes came up with a **NEW NUMBER SYSTEM** to count colossal numbers.

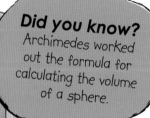

> **Did you know?**
> Archimedes worked out the formula for calculating the volume of a sphere.

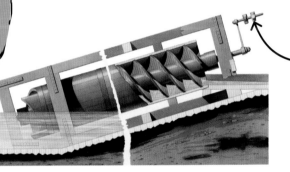

When a handle is turned, the blades rotate and scoop up water, moving it to a higher level.

Archimedes screw

By the time of his death in 212 BCE, Archimedes was the brains behind many **INVENTIONS**, including a **compound pulley, catapult, and war defences**. The best known was the *Archimedes screw*, a machine designed to carry heavy water to higher ground.

How he changed the world

Archimedes was way ahead of his time. As well as finding a new way of measuring volume and writing very large numbers – now known as standard notation – many more of his ideas and discoveries are still used today.

What came after...

In his book **Conics**, *Apollonius of Perga (c.262–190 BCE) examined conical sections, making new strides in the field of geometry. He was called the Great Geometer as a result.*

$$\frac{1}{x} + \frac{1}{y} = \frac{1}{n}$$

$$x^n + y^n = z^n$$

Among the first to use **SYMBOLS IN ALGEBRA**, *Greek mathematician Diophantus (201–285 BCE) wrote a series of books titled* Arithmetica, *which discussed algebraic equations.*

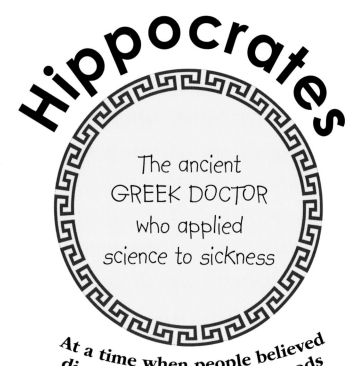

Hippocrates

The ancient GREEK DOCTOR who applied science to sickness

At a time when people believed diseases came from angry gods and evil spirits, Hippocrates used scientific treatments instead of superstitious traditions.

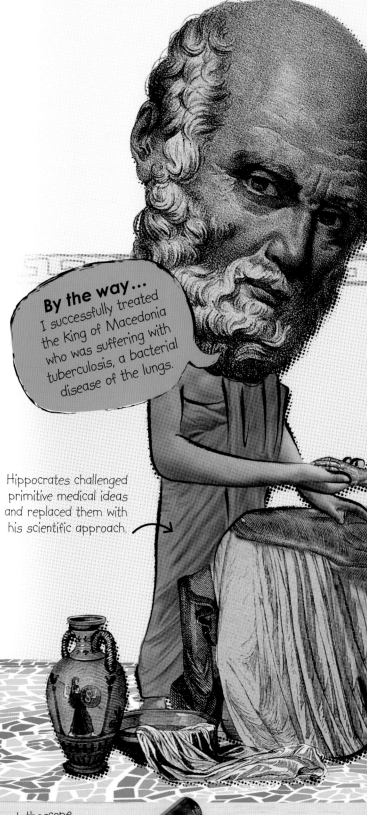

By the way...
I successfully treated the King of Macedonia who was suffering with tuberculosis, a bacterial disease of the lungs.

Hippocrates challenged primitive medical ideas and replaced them with his scientific approach.

Doctor's orders

Legend goes that Hippocrates was descended from the legendary Greek hero Hercules. Born in about 460 BCE on the island of Kos in Greece, Hippocrates enjoyed an excellent education. His father was a **DOCTOR** and Hippocates *learned medicine* from him. When Hippocrates himself became a doctor, he **established a school of medicine on Kos** and taught students everything he knew.

What came after...

Flemish physician Andreas Vesalius wrote one of the most important books on human anatomy – DE HUMANI CORPORIS FABRICA *– in 1543. It featured detailed anatomical illustrations.*

Laënnec's stethoscope was a simple tube, which helped to magnify sound.

In 1816, French physician René Laënnec invented the stethoscope. Replacing earlier paper versions, the LAËNNEC STETHOSCOPE *was made from wood with a single earpiece for doctors to listen to the heart and lungs.*

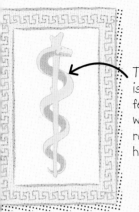

The Rod of Asclepius is a Greek symbol featuring a serpent wrapped around a rod. It represents healing and medicine.

This 11th-century illustration depicts the work of Hippocrates.

Hippocratic Corpus

The world's **OLDEST** set of medical books is the *Hippocratic Corpus*. This collection of about 70 documents **describes the symptoms and treatments of disease**. Although Hippocrates worked on these books, he did not write them all. Many Greek physicians taught themselves using these books.

This is a medieval Greek copy of the Hippocratic Oath.

Hippocratic Oath

Little is known of Hippocrates's death in about 370 BCE, but his influence impacts on medicine even today. The **Hippocratic Oath** is a **PROMISE** written in Greek times and attributed to Hippocrates, although he was not the author. It includes important ideas from Hippocrates, including *patient confidentiality and administering the best treatments*. This oath is still taken when new doctors start work.

How he changed the world

Did you know?
Hippocrates made careful note of his patients' symptoms in diagnosing diseases.

Hippocrates advanced medicine by suggesting diseases had natural causes that could be diagnosed and treated by science. This revolutionary idea was welcomed by other leading philosophers and physicians throughout Greece.

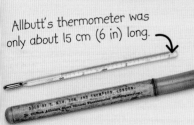

Allbutt's thermometer was only about 15 cm (6 in) long.

British doctor Thomas Allbutt invented a **POCKET-SIZED THERMOMETER** in 1866. His device was convenient to carry around and took very little time to read a person's temperature.

The **FIRST HUMAN HEART TRANSPLANT** was carried out by South African surgeon Dr Christiaan Barnard. He successfully operated on Louis Washkansky in 1967.

Astronomical achievements

Zhang Heng was born in China in 78 CE. He left home to study literature and found his gift for writing poetry. At the age of 30, he **became interested in astronomy** and was later appointed the **CHIEF ASTRONOMER** at the Han emperor's court. He observed the stars, mapped the planets, and tracked lunar eclipses. His cosmic contribution included *a catalogue of 2,500 stars and more than 100 constellations*.

Heng recognized that the Moon's shiny surface was the reflection of sunlight.

Zhang Heng

The Chinese poet whose far-flung INVENTIONS reached for the stars

Disaster warning

Concerned by earthquakes in China, Heng designed the **FIRST SEISMOMETER** in 132 CE. His **machine could detect movements 640 km (400 miles) away.** Heng also studied sets of numbers called magic squares, *placed the first mathematical grid system over a map*, and invented a device called an odometer to record the distance travelled by a wheeled cart.

During an earthquake, a ball from a dragon's head falls into the mouth of a frog to reveal the earthquake's direction.

How he changed...

The astronomical and mathematical innovations of Zhang Heng transformed ancient Chinese science.

the world

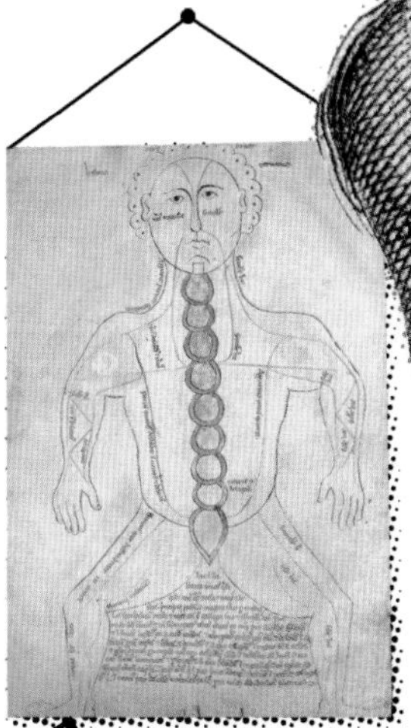

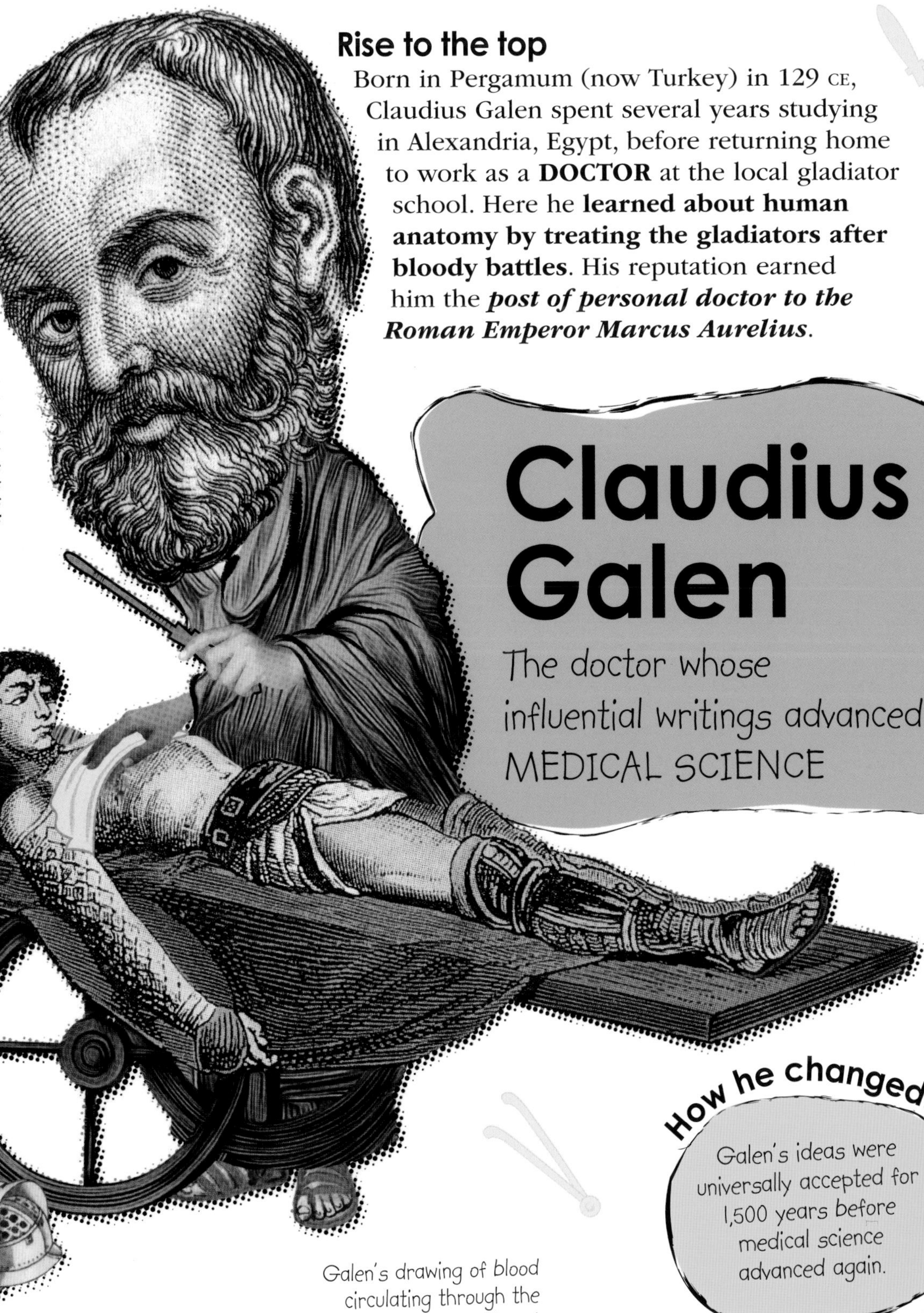

Rise to the top

Born in Pergamum (now Turkey) in 129 CE, Claudius Galen spent several years studying in Alexandria, Egypt, before returning home to work as a **DOCTOR** at the local gladiator school. Here he **learned about human anatomy by treating the gladiators after bloody battles**. His reputation earned him the *post of personal doctor to the Roman Emperor Marcus Aurelius*.

Galen's human anatomy chart

Claudius Galen

The doctor whose influential writings advanced MEDICAL SCIENCE

How he changed...

Galen's ideas were universally accepted for 1,500 years before medical science advanced again.

the world

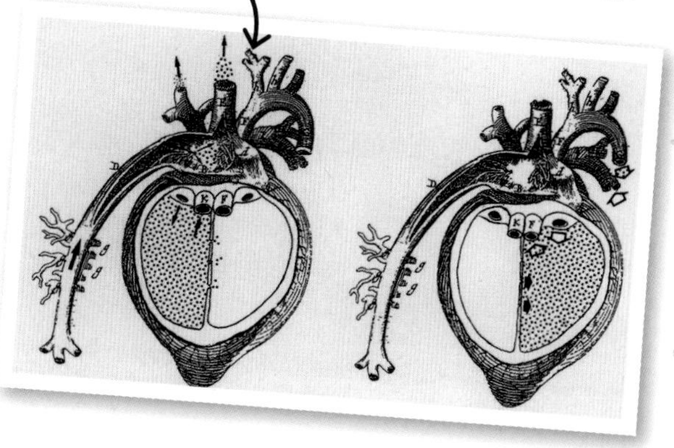

Galen's drawing of blood circulating through the human heart

Anatomy expert

Many of Galen's discoveries about the human body proved true. He realized the **arteries contain blood,** not air as previously thought. Galen was the first to understand that urine is created in the kidneys rather than the bladder. His *appetite for anatomical knowledge* made him compile the **HISTORY OF GREEK AND ROMAN MEDICINE**, combined with his own theories.

Al-Khwārizmī

The MATHEMATICS MARVEL with all the answers in algebra and algorithms

This Persian mathematician from the Middle Ages played a huge role in developing the most widely used number system in the world today.

Did you know?
The word algebra comes from the Arabic word "al-jabr". It was used in the title of al-Khwārizmī's first book.

House of Wisdom

Born in 780 CE in Baghdad, now Iraq, al-Khwārizmī was raised in a Persian family. He was summoned to Baghdad's new **Bayt al-Hikma**, meaning House of Wisdom, and soon became its director. This **CENTRE** of learning **translated important scientific works from around the world.**

Scholars from all over the world studied at the House of Wisdom.

Al-Khwārizmī invented the first quadrant for measuring time by observing the Sun and stars.

Arrival of algebra

Writing in Arabic, al-Khwārizmī compiled the world's first book about **ALGEBRA**, in which he explained practical symbols **used to express quantities and solve equations**. Algebra made it possible to solve different mathematical problems, *making trade, accounting, and tax collection easier*.

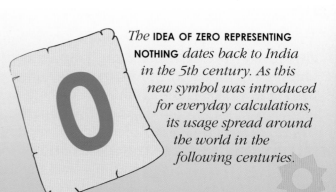

What came before...

One of the best known ancient mathematical works is the **RHIND MATHEMATICAL PAPYRUS** of Egypt. This document includes linear equations and answers written by a mathematician named Ahmes in about 1650 BCE.

The **IDEA OF ZERO REPRESENTING NOTHING** dates back to India in the 5th century. As this new symbol was introduced for everyday calculations, its usage spread around the world in the following centuries.

0

Understanding algorithms

In his second book, al-Khwārizmī used the **_Hindu-Arabic numerals of 0 and 1–9_**. This book was so popular that the Hindu-Arabic number system became the **standard across the Middle East and Europe**. Al-Khwārizmī's work also gave rise to the word **ALGORITHM**, which describes mathematical rules for calculation and computing.

The course of the River Nile was mapped by al-Khwārizmī.

Making his mark

Al-Khwārizmī did not stop at mathematics. A **_geography genius_** as well, he created a revised compilation of more than **2,000 coordinates for cities and landmarks** throughout Asia and Africa. In about 830 CE, he also helped to create a **WORLD MAP**.

Al-Khwārizmī helped popularize the Hindu-Arabic numerals, which are the basis of those we use today.

How he changed the world

Al-Khwārizmī's contribution to mathematics is remembered through the world's most common number system, as well as modern calculations that use algebra and algorithms.

Who came after...

During the 9th century, Arab philosopher **AL-KINDI** wrote widely on a range of scientific subjects, including his mathematical theory of parallel lines, and a four-volume work on the use of Indian numerals.

Italian mathematician **FIBONACCI** brought the popular system of Hindu-Arabic numerals to Europe from Africa, replacing the existing Roman numerals in the early 13th century.

Avicenna

The Islamic scholar who wrote one of the most INFLUENTIAL BOOKS in the history of medicine

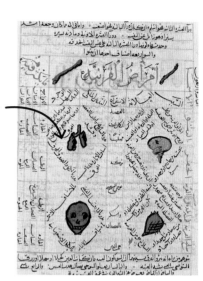

Avicenna's encyclopedia explains how to recognize and treat illnesses.

Gifted student

Born in about 980 CE in present-day Uzbekistan, Avicenna completed his studies in **MEDICINE** by the age of 16. He **cured the sultan of Bukhara** of a mysterious illness that baffled royal doctors. As a reward, he was granted access to the sultan's extensive library of rare manuscripts so that he could continue his research. Avicenna was an *influential scholar*, addressing questions about the relationship between religion and science.

Medical writings

Avicenna wrote **NUMEROUS BOOKS** during his lifetime. His five-volume encyclopedia, *The Canon of Medicine*, was a collection of all the medical knowledge known at that time, and became the **standard medical textbook** in both Europe and Asia.

How he changed... the world

Avicenna's writings laid the foundations of modern medical science. It was the basis of medical teaching in Europe up until the 17th century.

Great thinker

Averroës was born in 1126 in Córdoba, Spain. Growing up, he **studied science, religion, medicine, and philosophy**. Following in his grandfather's footsteps, he became **CHIEF JUDGE** of Seville in 1169. Two years later, Averroës returned to Córdoba to **study the forgotten work of Aristotle**, who was largely ignored by many thinkers at the time.

Averroës studied the work of Aristotle for many years.

Ancient Greek philosopher Aristotle

Averroës

The chief judge who became the greatest follower of ARISTOTLE'S WORK

This 20th-century statue of Averroës stands in his hometown of Córdoba.

Religion and science

Averroës's devotion to Islam and **skill as a mathematician and physician** showed it was possible to **combine religion and science** instead of seeing them as separate subjects. He also wrote his own **INFLUENTIAL** book called *General Medicine*. After he died in 1198, European universities honoured him by offering courses in his teachings.

How he changed...

Averroës reintroduced Aristotle's ideas on science and philosophy to the Western world, especially Christian and Jewish scholars in the 13th and 14th centuries.

the world

Fibonacci
Master MATHEMATICIAN of the Middle Ages

This Italian number cruncher shared a system, showed a sequence, and left a legacy.

By the way…
Some living creatures have the dimensions that correspond to the numbers in my sequence, including nautilus shells and chameleon tails.

Leonardo of Pisa

Fibonacci was born **Leonardo of Pisa** in Italy in about 1170. His father was a successful **MERCHANT** who took his son to trading posts in north Africa. Fibonacci learned about the *Hindu-Arabic numbers* when he visited Bugia, now in Algeria.

I II III IV V VI

Roman numbers featured complex and confusing letters of the alphabet.

1 2 ⊒ ⸲ 9 6

Hindu-Arabic numbers made calculations simpler.

New system

On his return to Pisa, Fibonacci introduced the Hindu-Arabic number system to Europe. This *counting system, which uses numerals 0 to 9*, is still used today. People could see its **advantages over existing Roman numbers**, so the Hindu-Arabic system was adopted across the **CONTINENT**.

What came before...

The scratched marks on this ancient bone may have been used to represent numbers.

In ancient times, numbers were counted out using simple TALLY SYSTEMS. Making marks on clay or lining up sticks and stones could represent animal herds or passing days.

1   2   3

4   5

About 5,000 years ago, the ancient Babylonians invented one of the first NUMBER SYSTEMS. These numerals were written as a series of symbols.

Fibonacci sequence

Fibbonacci is also known for a mathematical sequence of numbers in which *each number is found by adding together the last two*: 0, 1, 1, 2, 3, 5, 8, 13, 21, 34, 55, 89, and so on. These are called the **FIBONACCI NUMBERS**. Using this sequence for the sides of a square, a sequence of larger touching squares is formed. Then, by drawing a quarter circle between the corners of the sequence of Fibonacci squares, a **spiral shape is created**.

Clematis has eight petals

Buttercup has five petals

Daisy has 34 petals

Squares drawn using the Fibonacci numbers

A spiral forms where a quarter circle is drawn between the squares' corners.

Numbers in nature

Fibonacci's *sequence of numbers is seen all around us in nature*. Many flowers have the same number of petals as a number featured in the **FIBONACCI SEQUENCE**. Scientists also found the sequence in **plant leaves, pineapple scales, pine cones, and tree rings**.

How he changed the world

Fibonacci's introduction of Hindu-Arabic numbers brought mathematics to the masses. It is now a global mathematics language.

Did you know?
23 November is Fibonacci Day because in the month/date format (11/23), the numbers form the Fibonacci sequence: 1, 1, 2, 3.

What came after...

The **BINARY NUMBER SYSTEM** — a number system that uses only 0 and 1 – was invented by German mathematician Gottfried Leibniz in the 17th century. Today, computers store their programming as binary code, written in 0s and 1s.

In 1975, geometric shapes called **FRACTALS** were explained by Polish-born mathematician Benoit Mandelbrot. Sea shells are examples, producing a version of their main shape when divided down smaller.

Francis Bacon

The statesman who supported SCIENTIFIC THOUGHT

Francis Bacon banished old theories by bringing his own tried and tested formula to the scientific table.

Develop a theory

Make observations to closely examine a scientific subject.

Privileged upbringing

Born in London in 1561, Francis Bacon was **tutored at home** until he attended the University of Cambridge at the age of 12. He studied **LAW** but *found his course and tutors traditional and old-fashioned*.

Bacon's *Novum Organum* proposed a new approach to investigating the natural world.

After leaving Cambridge, Bacon studied law at Gray's Inn, London.

Great Seal of King James I

Strength to strength

Bacon became a *Member of Parliament* in 1581, and remained in parliament for almost four decades. In 1603, he was **KNIGHTED**, and went on to become the *Keeper of the Great Seal* – an important office that gave the king's approval to state documents.

What came after...

In 1672, English scientist Isaac Newton CARRIED OUT HIS GROUNDBREAKING EXPERIMENT *when he proved sunlight consists of different coloured light. This paved the way for modern optics.*

American scientist Benjamin Franklin PROVED LIGHTNING IS A FORM OF ELECTRICITY. *In 1752, he flew a kite during a storm, with a brass key tied to its string. Sparks flying off from the key showed electricity had passed through the kite.*

Scientific method

Against this backdrop of political success, Bacon **pursued his interest in science**. He called for a **NEW APPROACH** to the accepted ideas of the Greek philosopher Aristotle, and suggested laws of science were established by making observations, developing a theory, conducting experiments, and analyzing the results. In 1620, he described this in his book *Novum Organum* (New Instrument).

Test the theory through experiments and analyze results.

By the way...
After stuffing a chicken with snow, I discovered meat could be preserved in cold temperatures.

Scientists meeting at the Royal Society, London

Royal Society

Bacon died in 1626, but a group of scientists **adopted his new scientific method**. Together they founded the **ROYAL SOCIETY** in 1660, *an institute that promotes science*. It remains one of the most important scientific societies, leading by example for other international institutions.

How he changed the world

Although Francis Bacon did not invent anything specific, he turned science on its head with his new method based on observation and experiment. His approach was adopted by scientists around the world.

English chemist Joseph Priestley was a keen **EXPERIMENTER**. He discovered oxygen and eight other gases. In 1767, Priestley invented carbonated water, also known as fizzy water, by dissolving carbon dioxide in the liquid.

In 1804, French scientists Joseph Gay-Lussac and Jean-Baptiste Biot took to the skies – a record height of 7,016 m (23,018 ft) – in a hot-air balloon to **COLLECT AIR SAMPLES**. It was an amazing achievement at that time and one of the earliest studies of Earth's atmosphere.

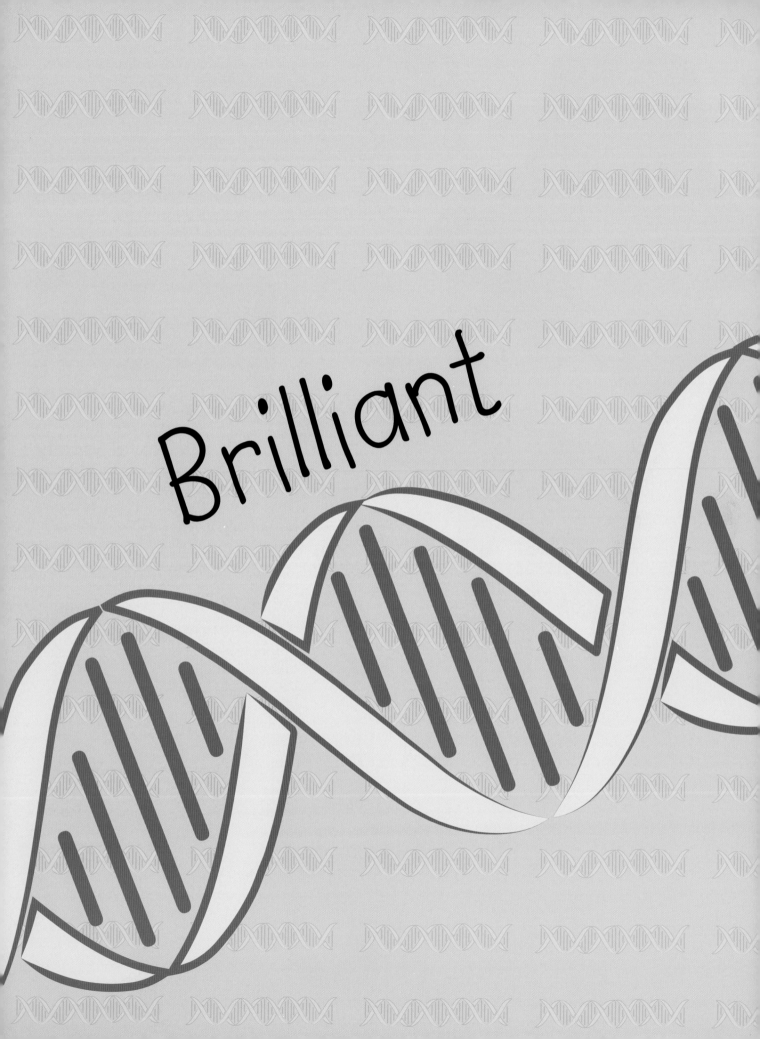

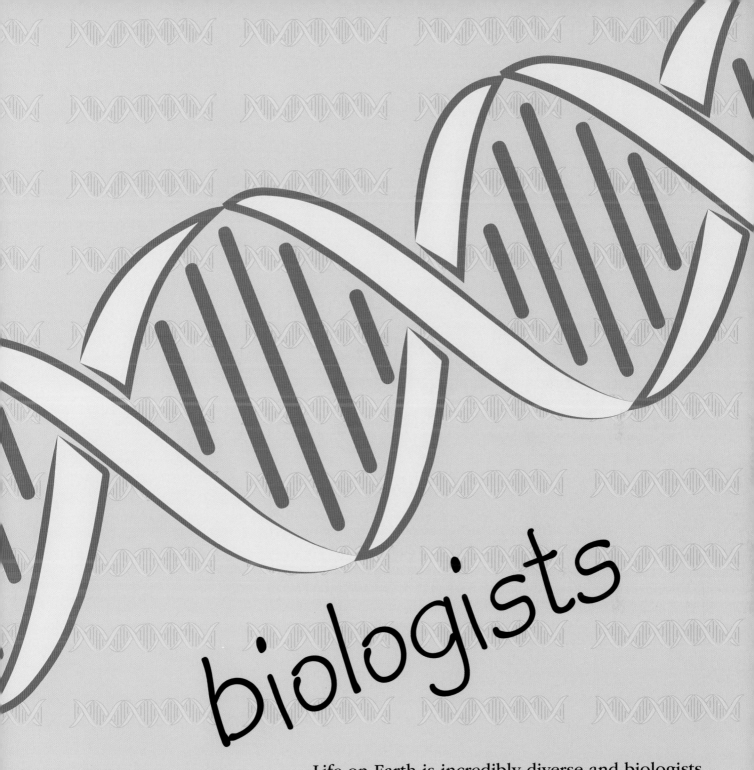

biologists

Life on Earth is incredibly diverse and biologists attempt to explore and understand the organisms that call our planet home. This branch of science covers a spectrum of studies – from anatomy to zoology – that helps us examine all kinds of plants and creatures. From early ideas of evolution to modern theories of genetics, biology has transformed the way we see ourselves and other life forms today.

Hildegard of Bingen

The singing NUN whose love of nature and flair for writing helped improve medieval medicine

Religious calling

Born in 1098 to a devoutly **religious** German family, Hildegard joined a Benedictine nunnery as a young girl, and later established her own **CONVENT**. Her *accomplishments in writing, poetry, and song* made Hildegard one of the most important female figures of the medieval church.

Medieval healthcare

Hildegard wrote about *botany, geology, healthcare, and science*. Her books offered advice on common medical problems together with a **catalogue** of alternative treatments and herbal remedies. Her work on **BLOOD CIRCULATION AND MENTAL ILLNESS** were considered advanced for the time. In 2012, Pope Benedict XVI formally recognized Hildegard as a saint. Her special feast day is celebrated annually on 17 September.

Hildegard identified many plants with medicinal qualities, such as tansy flowers.

How she changed...

Hildegard observed nature and wrote about the medicinal uses of plants, trees, and animals in her books.

the world

First discovery

Mary Anning was born into poverty in Lyme Regis, England. She received little education, and spent much of her time **combing the seashore for shells to sell**. In 1811, she and her brother found a **crocodile-like skeleton**. It was later identified as an **ICHTHYOSAUR**, or "fish lizard" – the first complete specimen ever found.

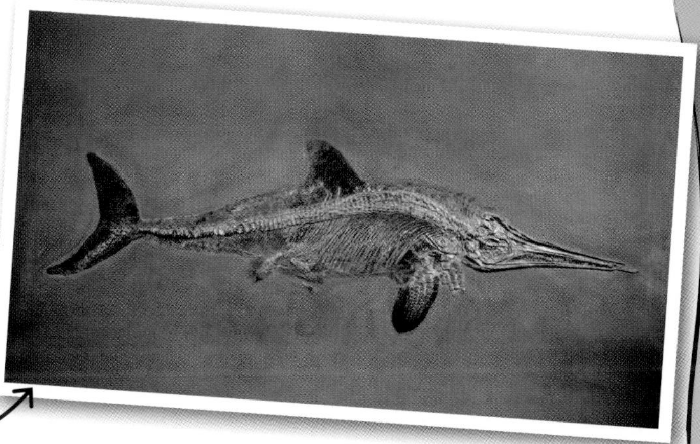

An ichthyosaur fossil embedded in rock.

By the way... At the age of one, I was struck by lightning but I survived.

Mary Anning

The amateur FOSSIL HUNTER who became a pioneering palaeontologist

Fossil finder

The cliffs near where Anning lived were **rich in prehistoric fossils**. She made many more **IMPORTANT FINDINGS**, including the first plesiosaur (a swimming reptile) and an early pterosaur (a flying reptile). Her discoveries challenged the religious view of creation and proved **how different creatures had lived and evolved over time**.

How she changed...

Anning's work provided critical evidence for palaeontologists who were developing theories about how life evolved on Earth.

the world

Fossil of an ammonite

Plesiosaur fossil

Seeing things

The bright sparks illuminating the mysterious world of LIGHT AND SIGHT

People have long been fascinated by what light is or how our eyes detect it. Here are some of the trailblazers who saw the light.

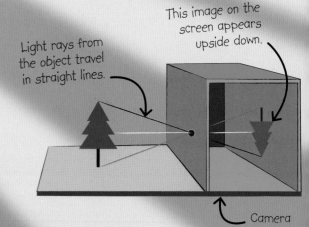

This image on the screen appears upside down.

Light rays from the object travel in straight lines.

Camera obscura

Alhazen

In the 10th century, this Islamic scholar wrote the highly influential **Book of Optics**. Through experiment, he proved that **vision occurs when light enters the eye**. He also discovered that refraction, or bending, of light is caused by light rays moving at varying speeds through different materials. Alhazen noticed that when light travels through the small hole in a **CAMERA OBSCURA**, the projection on the other side appears upside down. He therefore worked out that light rays must travel in straight lines.

Roger Bacon

This 13th-century English scholar placed great emphasis on **EXPERIMENT AND OBSERVATION** in science. Inspired by the work of Alhazen, he investigated the effects of mirrors and magnifying glasses. Bacon was one of the first people to suggest that **lenses could be used to improve a person's vision**. In 1267, Bacon gathered all his major ideas into a big book called **Opus Majus**.

16th-century spectacles

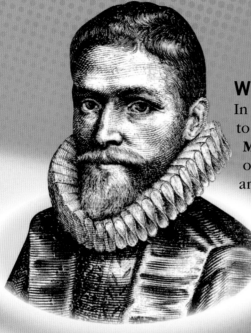

Willebrord Snell

In 1621, this Dutch astronomer used mathematics to show that it was possible to predict **HOW MUCH A RAY OF LIGHT WILL REFRACT**, or bend, when passing from one medium to another. This formula was called Snell's law and it forms the **basis of modern-day fibre optics**. This technology uses light energy to transmit data via fibre-optic cables (thin glass or plastic fibres that carry data) for many *wired phones and the Internet*.

Leeuwenhoek's
microscope

Antonie van Leeuwenhoek

Despite having no formal education, this 17th-century Dutch textile merchant became a **pioneer of microbiology**. Using a homemade microscope, he examined a drop of pond water, and was astonished to see *tiny organisms* – the **FIRST OBSERVED BACTERIA**. He built several hundred microscopes and went on to make many more discoveries, including blood cells.

Patricia Bath

This **laser scientist** is known for her innovative research in the areas of blindness prevention, treatment, and cure. Her achievements include the invention of a new device, the **LASERPHACO PROBE**, used in eye surgery to correct cataracts – a condition that can cause blindness. Patricia Bath was the *first female African-American doctor to patent a medical invention*.

Hooke designed the Monument to commemorate the Great Fire of London and the reconstruction of the city.

Great experimenter

Robert Hooke was a brilliant English scientist. **Interested in many subjects –** from mathematics and architecture to natural history, chemistry, and geology – he *conducted his experiments using scientific devices he had built himself*. Hooke also developed an important theory of elasticity in 1660, now known as **HOOKE'S LAW**.

How he changed...

Hooke's Micrographia revealed the natural world as never before, while his research helped to pave the way for better scientific devices.

the world

Robert Hooke

The scientist who studied the natural world through his MICROSCOPE

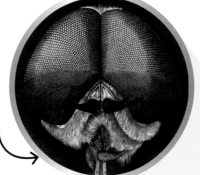

Hooke's illustration of a grey drone fly's head

By the way...
After the Great Fire of London in 1666, I worked with British architect Christopher Wren to rebuild the city.

Scientific bestseller

In his remarkable book, *Micrographia*, Hooke's own illustrations showed what he saw through **HIS MICROSCOPE**: a fly's eye, a bee's sting, and even a snowflake. He also **described a plant cell for the first time**.

Young botanist

Carl Linnaeus was born in Råshult, Sweden, in 1707. He was **fascinated by plants from an early age**. Frustrated by their *long and complicated names*, he became convinced that there was a simpler way of **NAMING** them.

Carl Linnaeus

The NATURALIST who invented the way we name living things

How he changed...

Linnaeus's classification system for organisms replaced chaos with order and still forms the backbone of the life sciences today.

the world

Linnaeus named thousands of life forms and classified them into clear groups.

Revolutionary change

Linnaeus published his important work *Systema Naturae* in 1735. It presented **a new way of classifying plants and animals**. Linnaeus grouped similar species together and gave each a **TWO-PART LATIN NAME**. The first name indicates the genus (or group) to which it belongs and the second part shows its species – such as the name for domestic cats, *Felis catus*.

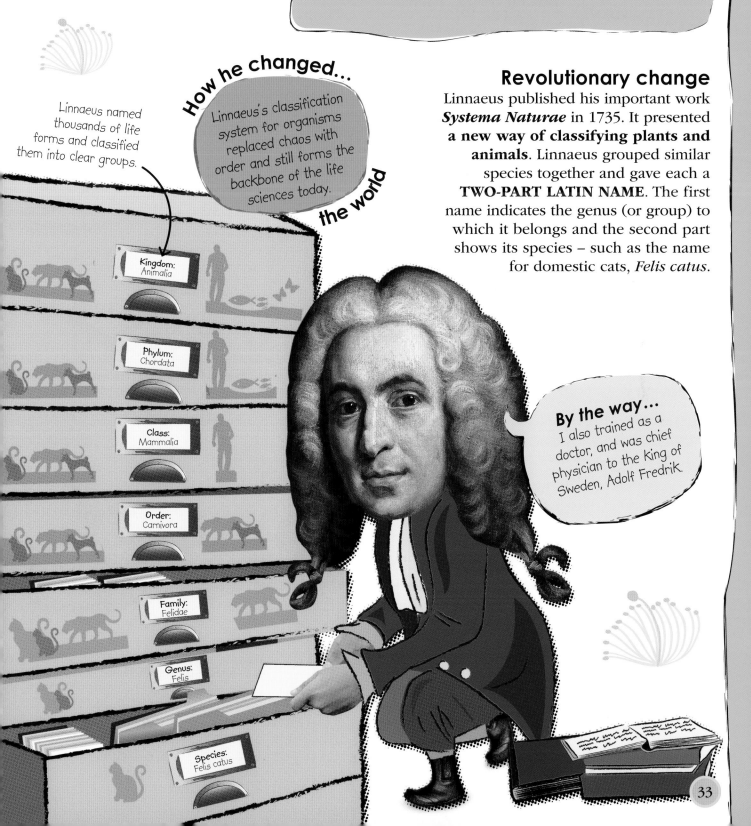

Kingdom: Animalia

Phylum: Chordata

Class: Mammalia

Order: Carnivora

Family: Felidae

Genus: Felis

Species: Felis catus

By the way...
I also trained as a doctor, and was chief physician to the King of Sweden, Adolf Fredrik.

Charles Darwin

PIONEER of evolutionary thinking

Darwin's theory that all living things have evolved from simple life forms made him one of the greatest biologists of all time.

Voyage of discovery

In 1831, Darwin joined a *five-year scientific expedition* as a **naturalist** on a ship called the HMS *Beagle*. He made notes and drew sketches of many of the plants and animals he came across. On the **GALÁPAGOS ISLANDS** in the Pacific, he was struck by how the beaks of the finches varied according to their diet.

Charles with his sister Catherine

The *Beagle* took nearly four years to reach the Galápagos Islands.

Love of nature

Born in 1809 in Shrewsbury, England, Charles Darwin began **studying medicine**, but he hated the sight of blood. He soon realized his *real passion* was for the **NATURAL WORLD** around him.

Did you know?
For Darwin's 25th birthday, the captain of the *Beagle* named a Chilean mountain after him.

Who came before...

French naturalist **JEAN-BAPTISTE LAMARCK** *noticed the similarities in the animals he studied. This led him to publish his theory in 1801, in which he stated that the gradual change of species occurs over time.*

British biologist **ALFRED RUSSEL WALLACE** *came up with a similar theory of evolution and shared it with Darwin in 1858, prompting Darwin to rush ahead and publish his ideas first.*

Survival of the fittest

After years of research, Darwin proposed his **theory of evolution by natural selection** in 1858. He argued that organisms with features that suit a particular environment are more likely to **SURVIVE** – these *features are naturally selected* and passed on to their offspring.

This sketch from Darwin's notebook shows life forms evolving like the branches of a tree.

By the way...
I worked on my theory in secret for more than 20 years; only a few of my closest friends knew about it.

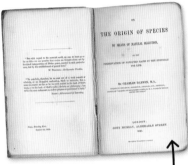

Darwin's *On the Origin of Species* has never been out of print since it was first published.

Controversy

Darwin's revolutionary book, *On the Origin of Species*, was published in 1859. His ideas **challenged the religious thinking of the time** – that God created all living things. However, by the time of his death in 1882, his theory was **WIDELY ACCEPTED** by the scientific community.

How he changed the world

Darwin's ideas provided an explanation for the diversity of life, and separated science from religion. His work is the basis of the natural sciences today.

Who came after...

In 1883, German biologist **AUGUST WEISMANN** *put forward his theory on how inheritance works. Weismann noted that characteristics do not blend in as was thought but were passed on through factors (now known as genes).*

British scientist **RICHARD DAWKINS** *wrote* The Selfish Gene, *an influential book about evolution that was published in 1976. He argued that natural selection acts on genes, selecting the fittest gene and making them more common in the population.*

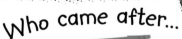

Gregor Mendel

The methodical monk who paved the way for GENETICS

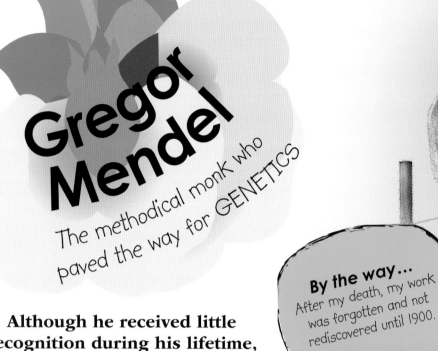

By the way...
After my death, my work was forgotten and not rediscovered until 1900.

Although he received little recognition during his lifetime, Gregor Mendel's experiments with pea plants launched the science of genetics.

Scientific monk

Gregor Mendel studied mathematics, physics, and philosophy before joining a monastery in 1843, aged 21. More interested in science than religion, he began **EXPERIMENTING WITH PEA PLANTS** in the *monastery's garden*. For thousands of years, people had bred animals and plants to produce offspring with the best traits, or features, but it was unreliable. Mendel wanted to find out **how physical characteristics were passed down the generations**.

Who came after...

In 1869, Swiss physician **FRIEDRICH MIESCHER** discovered an acid in the nuclei of red blood cells, now called DNA (deoxyribonucleic acid). Naming it nuclein, he proposed it might be the basis of heredity (the transfer of features from parents to offspring). Genes are made of DNA.

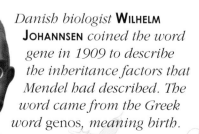

Danish biologist **WILHELM JOHANNSEN** coined the word gene in 1909 to describe the inheritance factors that Mendel had described. The word came from the Greek word genos, *meaning birth.*

Flower position	Flower colour	Plant height	Pea shape	Pea colour	Pod shape	Pod colour

Experiments

Mendel **focused on seven pea plant traits**: flower position and colour, plant height, pea shape and colour, and pod shape and colour. When he crossbred purple- and white-flowered plants, the **OFFSPRING** had purple flowers, but when he bred purple offspring with each other to create a *new generation*, some white flowers appeared again.

Parent plants

Each offspring has a set of instructions from each parent plant.

Purple is dominant so more flowers are this colour.

How the set of instructions mix determines the colour.

Inheritance laws

Mendel coined the terms **dominant and recessive**. He realized that each trait was controlled by a pair of **FACTORS** (now known as genes), one from each parent. The gene for purple flowers is dominant over the recessive gene for white flowers. For white flowers to appear, the *offspring must inherit the recessive gene* from both parents.

Did you know?
Mendel grew about 30,000 pea plants, methodically recording all his results.

How he changed the world

Before Mendel's work, nobody understood how traits were inherited. His experiments showed that they followed particular laws, now called Mendel's Laws.

In 1944, biologists **MACLYN MCCARTY**, **OSWALD AVERY**, *and* **COLIN MACLEOD** *provided the first evidence that the genetic material of living cells is made of DNA.*

Maclyn McCarty

One of the most important genetic ideas was unveiled in 2013 by Chinese-American scientist **FENG ZHANG**. *His gene-editing tool allows scientists to edit DNA in order to repair the faulty genes that cause diseases.*

Nettie Stevens

The GENETICS PIONEER who discovered what makes animals male or female

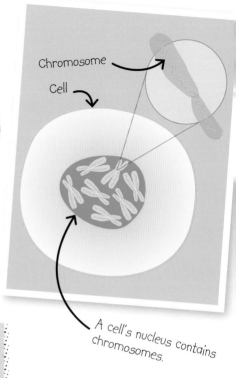

Chromosome

Cell

A cell's nucleus contains chromosomes.

Late starter

Born in Vermont, USA, in 1861, Nettie Stevens worked as a teacher before becoming a scientist in her thirties. At the time, *nobody understood what made an animal male or female*. Stevens began **RESEARCHING CHROMOSOMES**, the thread-like structures made of DNA inside a **cell's nucleus**.

How she changed...

Stevens solved a mystery that had long puzzled scientists by proving that an animal's sex is determined by genetics and not external factors.

the world

X and Y

By studying **mealworms**, Stevens found that males produce sperm containing either **X OR Y CHROMOSOMES**, while females produce eggs with **only X chromosomes**. If an egg is fertilized by a sperm with the Y chromosome, a male offspring is created. If the sperm has an X chromosome, then the offspring is female.

Curious zoologist

American geneticist Thomas Hunt Morgan became a professor of zoology in 1904. *Gregor Mendel* had already shown how **pea plants passed on different traits from one generation to the next**. Morgan set out to see if this **INHERITANCE** pattern also occurred in animals.

Morgan studied genes by breeding mutant white-eyed flies with normal red-eyed flies.

Thomas Hunt Morgan

The scientist who researched the role of CHROMOSOMES in inheritance

Flying high

Morgan **STUDIED FRUIT FLIES**. He discovered that they passed on dominant and recessive genes to their offspring. He found that genes are arranged on **chromosomes like beads on a string**, and that some are always *inherited together*. Two red-eyed flies could still produce white-eyed male offspring if the female carried the recessive gene for white eyes. His breakthrough discovery won him the Nobel Prize in Medicine in 1933.

By the way...
The fruit flies in my experiments were fed on ripe bananas, and many visitors found the smell overpowering!

Morgan stored thousands of fruit flies in bottles in his laboratory, known as the Fly Room.

How he changed...
Morgan's work on the link between chromosomes and inheritance paved the way for research into areas such as genetic diseases.

...the world

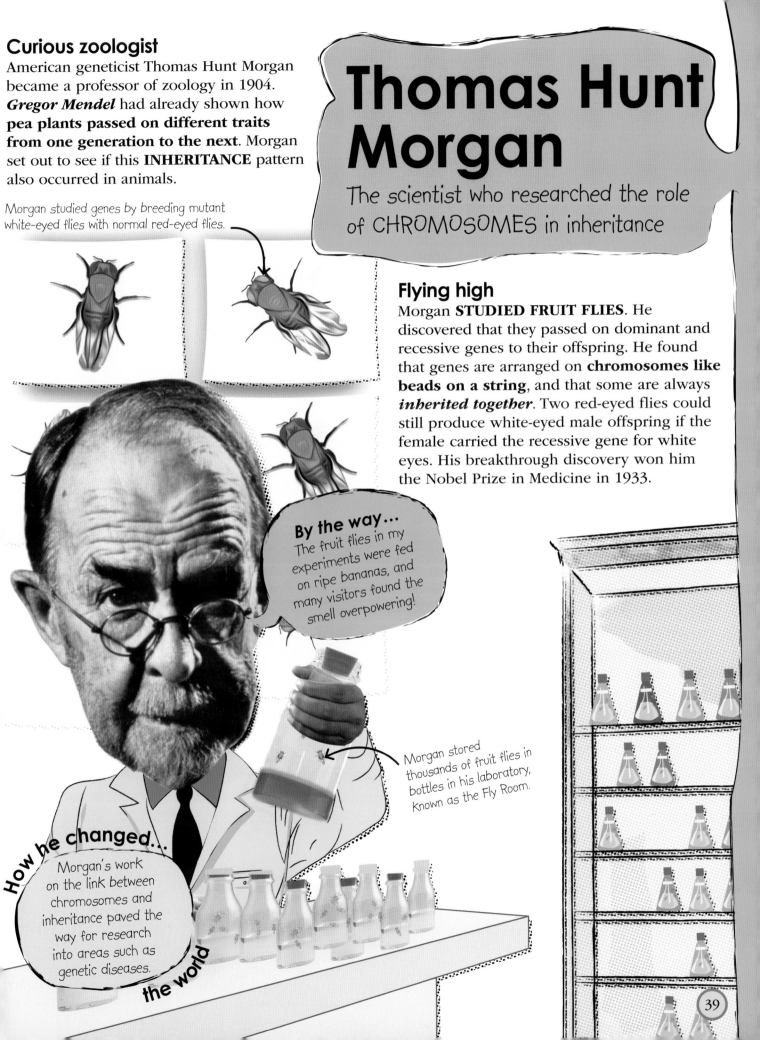

Alexander Fleming

Pioneer of PENICILLIN

The Scottish bacteriologist whose discovery of the first antibiotic has saved millions of lives.

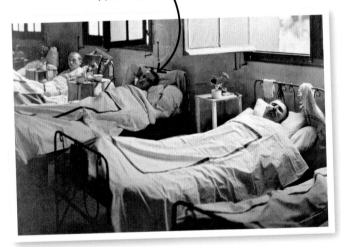
Wounded soldiers recover at a military hospital during World War I.

By the way... The laboratory at St Mary's Hospital, where I discovered penicillin, is now a public museum.

On the battlefield

Born in Scotland in 1881, Alexander Fleming moved to London in 1895. He went on to study medicine at St Mary's Hospital before working for the hospital **RESEARCH** team. During World War I, Fleming **worked in battlefield hospitals** in France, where he was upset by how many soldiers *died from infected wounds*.

Who came before...

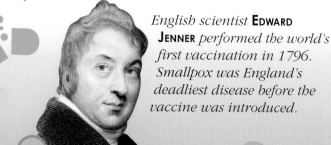

English scientist **EDWARD JENNER** *performed the world's first vaccination in 1796. Smallpox was England's deadliest disease before the vaccine was introduced.*

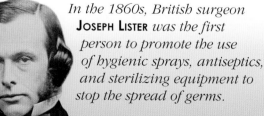

In the 1860s, British surgeon **JOSEPH LISTER** *was the first person to promote the use of hygienic sprays, antiseptics, and sterilizing equipment to stop the spread of germs.*

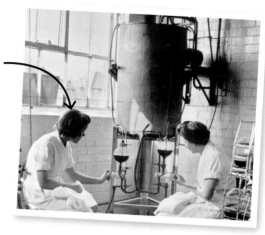

Penicillin-making mould in a petri dish

Technicians at work in a penicillin manufacturing laboratory

Bacteria blaster

After the war, Fleming returned to his research at St Mary's. In 1928, he noticed that the **STAPHYLOCOCCUS** bacteria he had been growing in his laboratory had become contaminated with mould. This mould formed a *bacteria-free zone* around itself. Fleming soon realized chemicals inside the mould could destroy bacteria. This anti-bacterial substance, named penicillin, was the **world's first antibiotic**.

Medical trials

Years of experiments with penicillin followed. When tests on human patients in 1941 **PROVED SUCCESSFUL**, American medicine companies began to produce penicillin in **large quantities**. The first supplies treated wounded World War II soldiers, *greatly reducing the death rate*.

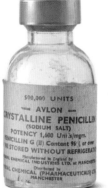

500,000 UNITS
AVLON
CRYSTALLINE PENICILLIN
(SODIUM SALT)
POTENCY 1,600 Units/mgm.
PENICILLIN G (II) Content 96% or over
BE STORED WITHOUT REFRIGERATION
Manufactured in England by
IMPERIAL CHEMICAL INDUSTRIES LTD. at MANCHESTER
Distributed by
IMPERIAL CHEMICAL (PHARMACEUTICALS) LTD.
MANCHESTER

Prized penicillin

Penicillin became *the main treatment for many diseases*, including gangrene, diphtheria, and pneumonia. Fleming was **KNIGHTED** in 1944, and he jointly received the **Nobel Prize in Medicine** a year later.

Did you know?
Asteroid 91006 Fleming in the Asteroid Belt is named in honour of Alexander Fleming.

How he changed the world

Fleming's groundbreaking discovery led to the introduction of other antibiotics to attack germs, fungi, and parasites. One unexpected moment in the laboratory made our planet a healthier and safer place.

Who came after...

In 1943, American microbiologists **SELMAN WAKSMAN** *and* **ALBERT SCHATZ** *discovered streptomycin, a new antibiotic used to cure tuberculosis – an infectious disease that mainly affects the lungs.*

Selman Waksman

During the 1970s, American chemist **GERTRUDE B ELION** *developed acyclovir, the first widely available antiviral drug, which helped combat the virus that causes chickenpox and shingles.*

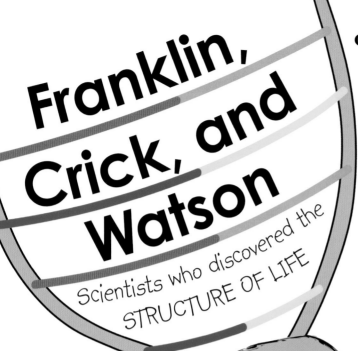

Franklin, Crick, and Watson

Scientists who discovered the STRUCTURE OF LIFE

Cracking the DNA model was a combined effort, but while Crick and Watson found themselves in the limelight, Franklin was left in the shadows.

Franklin's Photo 51 helped Crick and Watson complete the DNA structure.

DNA is a chemical code inside every creature's cells, giving instructions on how cells work and grow.

By the way... Personality clashes with some of my laboratory colleagues earned me the nickname "the dark lady of DNA".

Rosalind Franklin

Born in London in 1920, Rosalind Franklin set her heart on science. She gained a PhD in 1945 before moving to Paris to study the **CRYSTAL STRUCTURES** of chemicals using X-rays. By the 1950s, many scientists were studying **deoxyribonucleic acid (DNA)** – the chemical found inside cells of living things. Back at King's College laboratory in London, Franklin took *X-ray photographs of DNA crystals*. In one of these, which she labelled Photo 51, she spotted a two-part spiral, called a double helix structure.

The double helix structure of DNA resembles a spiral staircase.

Who came before...

In 1866, German biologist **ERNST HAECKEL** made a breakthrough when he suggested that the genetic material inherited between generations is located in the nucleus of each body cell.

Englishman **WILLIAM HENRY BRAGG** and Australian-born **WILLIAM LAWRENCE BRAGG** used X-rays to study crystal structures and explain diffraction in 1915. They became the first father and son team to share a Nobel Prize.

William Lawrence Bragg

Francis Crick and James Watson

At the same time as Franklin, English scientist Francis Crick and American scientist James Watson were working on their own model of the structure of **DNA**. They were shown Photo 51 by Franklin's colleague Maurice Wilkins. Together with their own work, this photograph helped them ***confirm the double helix structure*** and meant the duo could complete their model, called **the secret of life** in 1953.

Recognition

Franklin died in 1958, probably as a result of **radiation exposure** from X-rays. ***Crick, Watson, and Maurice Wilkins*** went on to win the Nobel Prize in Physiology or Medicine in 1962 for their DNA structure. Franklin received **NO CREDIT** as the prize can only be given to living scientists.

DNA can be used to identify any individual as everyone has their own unique chemical code.

How they changed the world

The structure of DNA proved a monumental moment in scientific history, impacting on genetic development, medical research, and forensic analysis.

Did you know?

Rosalind Franklin is now receiving recognition for her contribution to understanding DNA, with colleges and scholarships in her name.

What came after...

FORENSIC SCIENCE *has evolved thanks to DNA. The police can find a criminal using DNA traces left at the crime scene, in things such as blood, saliva, skin, and hair.*

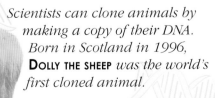

Scientists can clone animals by making a copy of their DNA. Born in Scotland in 1996, **DOLLY THE SHEEP** *was the world's first cloned animal.*

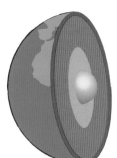

Inge Lehmann

This Danish scientist worked out that Earth's inner core is solid and not liquid.

The GEOLOGIST who studied earthquakes and discovered Earth's deepest secret

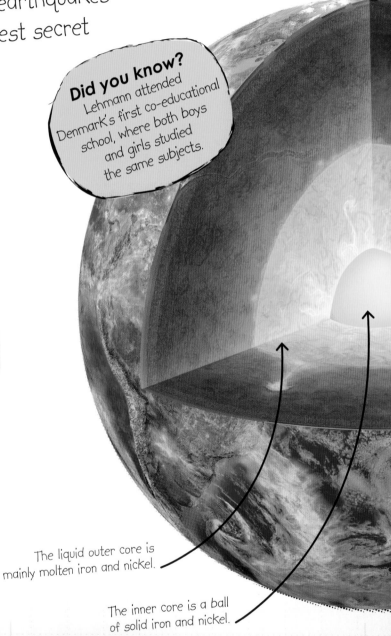

Did you know?
Lehmann attended Denmark's first co-educational school, where both boys and girls studied the same subjects.

Beneath the surface

Inge Lehmann's career in **SEISMOLOGY** – the study of earthquakes and the seismic waves they produce – began in 1925 when she became **responsible for analyzing data from seismic observatories**. Seismic waves travel at varying speeds through different layers of Earth, *revealing clues about Earth's inner mysteries*.

The liquid outer core is mainly molten iron and nickel.

The inner core is a ball of solid iron and nickel.

Who came before...

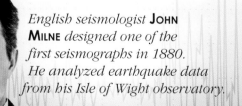

English seismologist **JOHN MILNE** *designed one of the first seismographs in 1880. He analyzed earthquake data from his Isle of Wight observatory.*

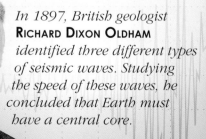

In 1897, British geologist **RICHARD DIXON OLDHAM** *identified three different types of seismic waves. Studying the speed of these waves, he concluded that Earth must have a central core.*

A brilliant discovery

At the time, scientists believed Earth consisted of a liquid core surrounded by a solid mantle. In 1929, a large **EARTHQUAKE** in New Zealand sent shockwaves around the world. Using basic technology, Lehmann analyzed the data and noticed that **some seismic waves appeared to be bouncing off a boundary within Earth's core**. In 1936, she published her theory that *Earth's centre consists of a solid inner core surrounded by a liquid outer core*.

By the way...
Without a computer, I recorded my data on slips of cardboard and stored them in old cereal boxes.

Lehmann was the first woman to receive the William Bowie Medal.

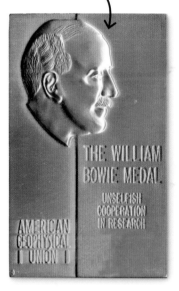

THE WILLIAM BOWIE MEDAL

UNSELFISH COOPERATION IN RESEARCH

AMERICAN GEOPHYSICAL UNION

Leading expert

Lehmann established herself as an **expert on Earth's upper mantle**. In later years, *she discovered another boundary*, about 220 km (137 miles) below Earth's surface, now known as the **LEHMANN DISCONTINUITY**. During her lifetime, Lehmann received many awards, including the American Geophysical Union's William Bowie Medal in 1971.

How she changed the world

Inge Lehmann's discovery helped to redefine how our planet was studied. She was also a pioneer of equal rights at a time when there were few opportunities for female scientists.

What came after...

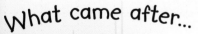

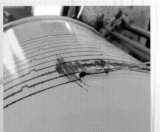

In 1935, seismologists Charles Richter and Beno Gutenberg developed **A SYSTEM FOR MEASURING EARTHQUAKES**, *using a scale of 0–10. The higher the number, the stronger the earthquake. A seismograph is used for recording the earthquake's seismic waves.*

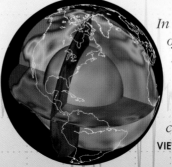

In 2017, with the help of the powerful Titan supercomputer and seismic data generated by 253 earthquakes, Princeton University researchers created a detailed **3D VIEW OF EARTH'S INTERIOR.**

Skilled inventor

In 1957, English scientist James Lovelock invented the electron capture detector to *measure the amounts of chemical pollutants* in water, air, and soil. He found evidence of **contamination in plants and animals**. This showed that compounds known as CFCs, which were used in spray cans and other items, were **DESTROYING EARTH'S OZONE LAYER** – the layer that shields us from the Sun's harmful ultraviolet rays. CFCs were eventually banned.

This instrument was designed by Lovelock in the 1960s to measure CFC concentrations.

How he changed...

Lovelock sparked research into how human activity was affecting our planet, and became an inspiration for the environmental movement.

the world

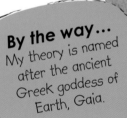

By the way...
My theory is named after the ancient Greek goddess of Earth, Gaia.

Living Earth

Lovelock is most famous for his **GAIA THEORY**, a new way of thinking about *Earth as one giant organism*. Working with American microbiologist Lynn Margulis, he proposed that Earth's atmosphere, oceans, land, and organisms interact to **maintain conditions suitable for life** – much as warm-blooded animals regulate body temperature.

James Lovelock

The ENVIRONMENTALIST whose vision of Earth as a vast, living organism changed the way we see our world

Keeling collected air samples in flasks like this to analyze CO_2.

I-216

Fossil fuel debate

During the 1950s, American Charles David Keeling designed instruments for measuring **CARBON DIOXIDE** (CO_2) levels in *Earth's atmosphere*. At the time, nobody knew whether CO_2 – **released by the burning of fossil fuels** in factories and through the use of cars – ended up in the atmosphere or not.

How he changed...

Keeling's data proved a clear link between human activity and global warming, alerting politicians to the problem.

the world

Charles David Keeling

The CHEMIST who measured carbon dioxide levels in Earth's atmosphere and raised the alarm over the planet's rising temperature

Iconic graph

In 1958, Keeling began measuring CO_2 levels at the South Pole and at the summit of the Mauna Loa volcano in Hawaii. Tracking his data on a graph, known as the **KEELING CURVE**, he discovered that the *levels rose each year*. This led to warnings about how rising CO_2 levels could lead to **a catastrophic increase in Earth's temperature**.

The Keeling Curve plots changing CO_2 levels in Earth's atmosphere.

CO₂ concentration

390
380
370
360
340
320
310

1960   1970   1990   2000   2010

Year

Medical masterminds

The super scientists who made breakthroughs in HEALTHCARE

These trailblazers transformed medicine, bringing the treatments and cures to save the lives of millions.

Variola is the virus that causes smallpox, producing fever and rashes.

Edward Jenner

In the 18th century, England's deadliest disease was **SMALLPOX**. English doctor Edward Jenner found that **introducing a mild dose of cowpox** (a similar, less dangerous disease) prepared the human body to fight smallpox. In 1796, Jenner's smallpox vaccine became *the world's first successful vaccine*, eventually helping to wipe out the disease.

Jonas Salk

American microbiologist Jonas Salk **developed the first effective polio vaccine** after years of medical research and testing. Declared safe in 1955, more than **200 MILLION VACCINES** were administered in the USA in the following two years. Polio, which usually affects young children, has now been *eradicated in all but a handful of countries*.

The polio virus attacks the spinal cord, leading to paralysis.

Paul Ehrlich

German doctor Paul Ehrlich along with his assistant Sahachiro Hata discovered that a chemical containing **arsenic** could work as an effective treatment for syphilis, a bacterial disease. Ehrlich established that *chemicals could be used to treat diseases*, naming this process **CHEMOTHERAPY**. His work on the human immune system won him the Nobel Prize in Physiology in 1908.

Treponema pallidum causes syphilis.

The deadly HIV virus has killed millions of people.

Françoise Barré-Sinoussi

In 1983, French virologist Françoise Barré-Sinoussi discovered that HIV (Human Immunodeficiency Virus) *attacks the human body's immune system*, causing AIDS (Acquired Immunodeficiency Syndrome) – a disease that weakens a person's ability to fight infection. Her work led to an **increasing awareness of HIV and AIDS, and to better treatments for patients**. She was awarded the Nobel Prize in Medicine in 2008.

Joshua Lederberg

American geneticist Joshua Lederberg studied **bacteria molecules** and *discovered they could transfer genes between each other*. For his work on the genetic arrangement of bacteria, he shared the 1958 Nobel Prize in Medicine. His work laid the foundations for **GENETIC ENGINEERING**, the scientific modification of genetic material inside living things.

E. coli, one of the bacteria studied by Lederberg

Clever chemists

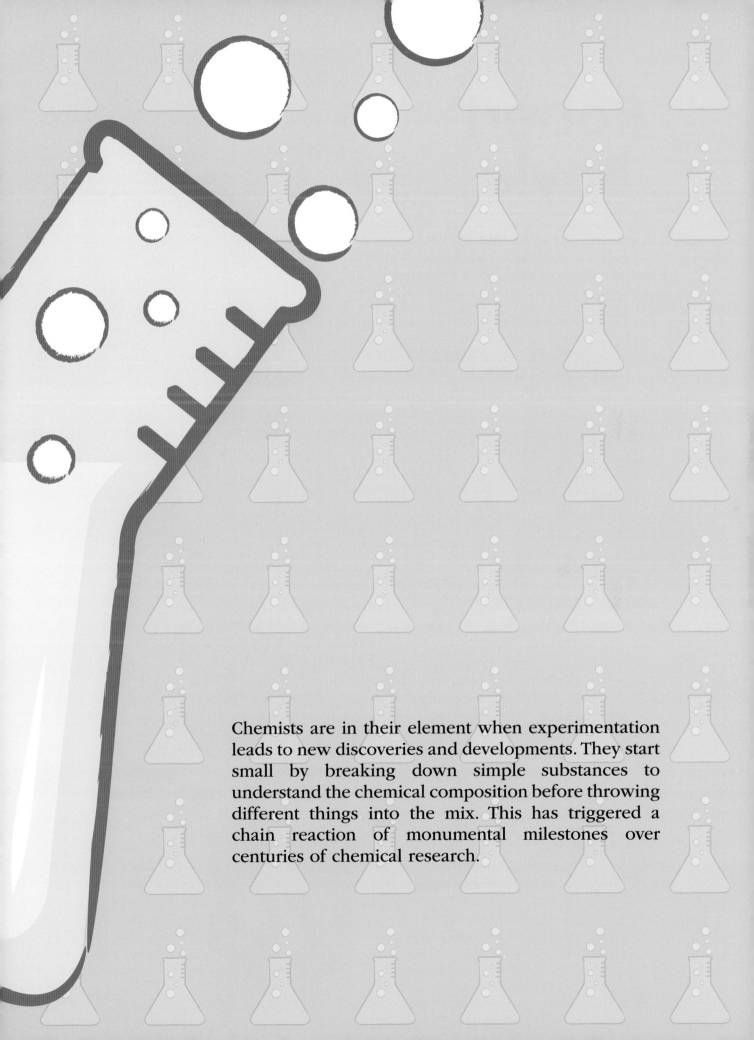

Chemists are in their element when experimentation leads to new discoveries and developments. They start small by breaking down simple substances to understand the chemical composition before throwing different things into the mix. This has triggered a chain reaction of monumental milestones over centuries of chemical research.

Robert Boyle

By the way...
As an alchemist, I was unsuccessful in finding the legendary Philosopher's Stone, which was said to turn any metal into gold.

The first MODERN CHEMIST

This aristocratic author from Ireland advanced modern chemistry with the first law of gases.

A privileged life

Born in 1627 at **Lismore Castle** in Ireland, Boyle's aristocratic family sent him on a **TOUR OF EUROPE** when he was 12. On his return in 1644, he began writing on a wide range of subjects. Although a religious person, Boyle's books and essays emphasized *scientific and mathematical studies*.

Ireland

Switzerland

France

Italy

Touring European countries such as France, Switzerland, and Italy was a traditional part of a wealthy child's education.

Productive period

In 1649, Boyle started **EXPERIMENTING** with elements and chemicals. He later moved to Oxford to set up a laboratory. Although he never held any post, Boyle *shared ideas and showcased experiments* in a group called the **Experimental Philosophy Club**, alongside important people such as British physician and philosopher John Locke and English architect Christopher Wren.

Who came before...

In the 8th century, alchemist GEBER was the first to suggest the existence of a Philosopher's Stone that could create gold from metals. Many medieval scientists spent their lives trying to create one.

Swiss alchemist PARACELSUS believed the Universe was made up of metals controlled by God. To make medical progress, he suggested doctors should study nature and conduct experiments.

Boyle's law

Boyle employed a skilled student named Robert Hooke as his assistant. Together they invented an air pump to examine **pneumatics**, the area of physics studying gas behaviour. They *made a breakthrough discovery* – at a constant temperature, increasing pressure on a gas squeezes it and decreases its volume, and vice versa. Published in 1662, **BOYLE'S LAW** became the first gas law.

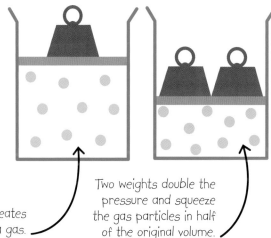

A single weight creates low pressure in a gas.

Two weights double the pressure and squeeze the gas particles in half of the original volume.

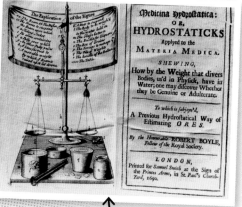

Boyle's book *Medicina Hydrostatica*

The air pump helped Boyle to examine the behaviour of gases.

Lasting legacy

Boyle was at the heart of the **SCIENTIFIC REVOLUTION** in which scientists *developed new theories and principles about the natural world*. After his death in 1691, Boyle's research papers were given to the **Royal Society**, a scientific research institution born out of the Experimental Philosophy Club.

How he changed the world

Robert Boyle replaced the superstitions of alchemy with real chemistry, using his own experiments to establish new laws of science.

Did you know?
The Boyle Lectures were started in 1692 to discuss the relationship between religion and science. They were revived in the 21st century.

Who came after...

French chemist **ANTOINE LAVOISIER** also studied gases, mainly exploring the fields of combustion and respiration. He went on to give the element oxygen its name.

The second gas law, called *Charles's Law*, is named after French chemist **JACQUES CHARLES**. It states that as the temperature increases, particles inside a gas move faster and the volume increases.

Laboratory life

Scottish scientist Joseph Black studied medicine at the University of Glasgow where Dr William Cullen gave chemistry lectures. Black **worked as Cullen's laboratory assistant** on many research projects, which **ignited his own interest in chemistry**. Black's work led to the discoveries of magnesium, bicarbonates, and a gas he called fixed air, which turned out to be **CARBON DIOXIDE**.

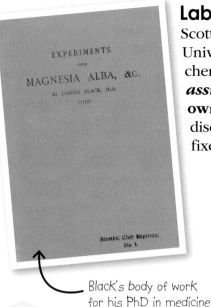

Black's body of work for his PhD in medicine

The heat is on

In the late 1700s, Black carried out an **IMPORTANT EXPERIMENT**. He filled one container with solid water (ice) and another one with liquid water (with a drop of alcohol to stop it from freezing). At this point, the temperature of the containers was exactly the same. After leaving them to warm up, he discovered that the **temperature of the liquid water and alcohol rose**, but the temperature of the ice container stayed the same, even though the ice was melting. He realized the heat that had increased the temperature of the liquid mixture had instead been used up just melting the ice in the frozen container. This experiment showed the **difference between heat and temperature**.

Even as the ice melted, the temperature stayed the same.

Liquid water mixed with alcohol got warmer.

Joseph Black

The British CHEMIST who turned up the heat with a series of discoveries

How he changed...

Black's experiments led to groundbreaking theories about stored heat, called latent heat, and made it clear that heat was different from temperature.

the world

Benjamin Franklin inspired Priestley to pursue his interest in science.

Joseph Priestley

The British MINISTER who brought a breath of fresh air to experimental science

Preacher and teacher

Born in Yorkshire in 1733, Joseph Priestley originally became a **CLERGYMAN** and **language tutor**. A friendship with American scientist Benjamin Franklin led Priestley to publish his opinion that *new findings were more important than past beliefs*.

Foot on the gas

On 1 August 1774, Priestley conducted an experiment using a chemical called mercuric oxide, and made his **MOST IMPORTANT DISCOVERY**. He *obtained a colourless gas, which later came to be known as oxygen*. Priestley also isolated nitrous oxide, better known as **laughing gas**.

In his experiment, using a burning lens, Priestley focused sunlight on mercuric oxide inside an inverted glass container.

The colourless gas released caused a flame to burn with more intensity, which led Priestley to investigate it further.

How he changed...

Joseph Priestley became a big name in experimental science by discovering 10 gases.

the world

55

Alessandro Volta

The genius who created CONTINUOUS CURRENT

This Italian inventor's enthusiasm for electricity produced the world's ultimate power source.

The taller the stack, the more electric current is generated.

Bright spark

As a teenager, Alessandro Volta corresponded with physicist Giambattista Beccaria. He encouraged Volta to **learn by experimentation**. In 1791, Volta's friend *Luigi Galvani* noticed that a frog's legs twitched when they touched different metals, but mistook this for electricity inside living cells. Volta realized the frog was the conductor for electricity generated by the metal, so he experimented with what he called **METALLIC ELECTRICITY**.

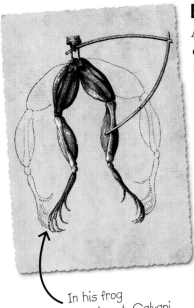

In his frog experiment, Galvani discovered that a pair of different metals produced electricity.

Cardboard soaked in acid or salt water is called the electrolyte.

Zinc and copper discs are called electrodes.

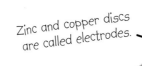

What came after...

Before inventing the famous Bunsen burner, German scientist Robert Bunsen designed the zinc-carbon cell, called the **BUNSEN BATTERY**, in 1841.

In 1859, French physicist Gaston Planté invented the lead-acid battery, the world's *first* **MASS-PRODUCED RECHARGEABLE BATTERY**.

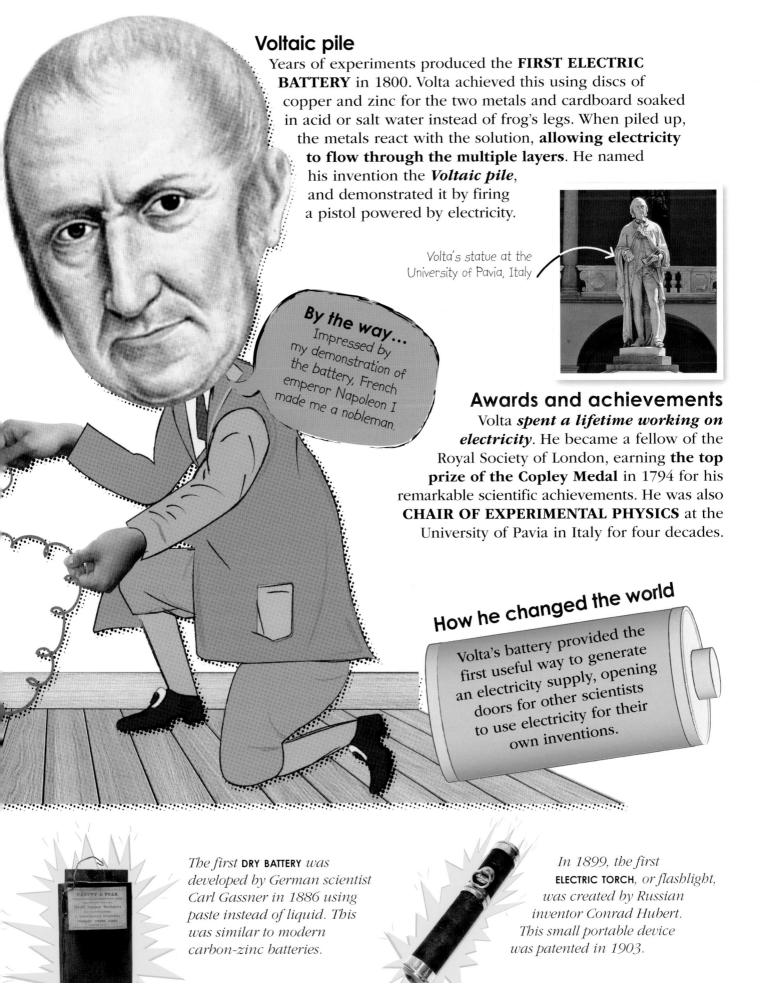

Voltaic pile

Years of experiments produced the **FIRST ELECTRIC BATTERY** in 1800. Volta achieved this using discs of copper and zinc for the two metals and cardboard soaked in acid or salt water instead of frog's legs. When piled up, the metals react with the solution, **allowing electricity to flow through the multiple layers**. He named his invention the *Voltaic pile*, and demonstrated it by firing a pistol powered by electricity.

Volta's statue at the University of Pavia, Italy

By the way... Impressed by my demonstration of the battery, French emperor Napoleon I made me a nobleman.

Awards and achievements

Volta *spent a lifetime working on electricity*. He became a fellow of the Royal Society of London, earning **the top prize of the Copley Medal** in 1794 for his remarkable scientific achievements. He was also **CHAIR OF EXPERIMENTAL PHYSICS** at the University of Pavia in Italy for four decades.

How he changed the world

Volta's battery provided the first useful way to generate an electricity supply, opening doors for other scientists to use electricity for their own inventions.

The first **DRY BATTERY** was developed by German scientist Carl Gassner in 1886 using paste instead of liquid. This was similar to modern carbon-zinc batteries.

In 1899, the first **ELECTRIC TORCH**, or flashlight, was created by Russian inventor Conrad Hubert. This small portable device was patented in 1903.

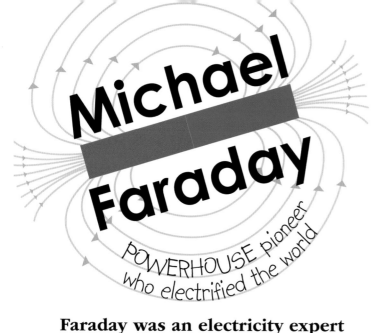

Michael Faraday

POWERHOUSE pioneer who electrified the world

Faraday was an electricity expert who brought power to the people, becoming one of the biggest names in scientific history.

Current is passed through the metal wire.

Bar of magnet in a bowl filled with mercury

Motor running

Faraday's experiments specialized in combining electricity and magnetism, called **electromagnetism**. This was how he came to make history in 1821 by inventing the **FIRST ELECTRIC MOTOR**. When a magnet is moved through a wire coil, it produces an electric current. The ability to harness electromagnetic energy had the *potential to replace machines powered by horses, steam, and water*.

Faraday's transformer

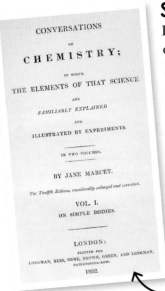

Set for science

Despite leaving school at the age of 13 and working as a bookbinder, **Michael Faraday** became one of the most important scientists ever. He spent his free time reading books, and after attending a lecture by leading chemist Humphry Davy in 1812, *Faraday became interested in science*. He carried out his own experiments at the back of the bookshop, and eventually became Davy's assistant at the **ROYAL INSTITUTION** in London.

Jane Marcet's 600-page book *Conversations on Chemistry* inspired Faraday to pursue chemistry.

Did you know?
In 1858, Prince Albert gave Faraday a house at Hampton Court Palace for his contributions to science.

Who came after...

Inspired by Faraday, Scottish scientist **JAMES CLERK MAXWELL** discovered in 1862 that electricity and magnetism were the same force, and that light was a form of electromagnetic wave.

American inventor **THOMAS ALVA EDISON** set up the first commercial power plant in New York City, USA, in 1882. It is considered the world's first station to generate electricity.

Electromagnetic inventions

Years of experimentation led to **two more inventions**. The **TRANSFORMER** was an iron ring designed to reduce electric voltages for safe use in electrical equipment. The **DYNAMO** was the first electric generator, using *magnets to convert movement into electricity*. In Faraday's design, a copper disc is rotated manually to pass between the poles of a magnet, producing an electric current in the copper.

By the way...
I loved to share my knowledge of science with everyone and gave Christmas Day lectures at the Royal Institution, a tradition that has continued with other scientists.

1870s model of Faraday's dynamo

How he changed the world

Faraday's research can be seen all around us. Every piece of electrical equipment features a motor, while transformers and generators provide power for us.

After producing electromagnetic waves in his laboratory, German physicist **HEINRICH HERTZ** became the first person to send and receive radio waves in 1888.

American **EDITH CLARKE** was the first female electrical engineer and professor of electrical engineering. She studied electrical power sources and documented her findings on power distribution in many books.

Louis Pasteur

MASTERMIND of microbiology

Louis Pasteur battled bacteria to save thousands of lives, placing health and hygiene at the forefront of modern science.

This 19th-century machine was used to pasteurize milk bottles.

Pasteurization

In the early 1860s, Pasteur's research showed that **heating a liquid to 55°C (131°F)** killed bacteria without changing the liquid's taste. This process, later called **pasteurization**, was adopted by the dairy industry; milk is **PURIFIED** by pasteurization before it is ready for sale.

Patients infected with rabies queued for treatment.

Fresh findings

In the early 19th century, people believed **infections appeared from nowhere**. Born in 1822, French chemistry professor Louis Pasteur **EXAMINED** different types of infections. He proved that *they are caused by germs, including some kinds of bacteria.*

Did you know?
Established in 1887 by the great scientist himself, the Pasteur Institute in France is still at the forefront in the battle against infectious diseases.

What came after...

Carbolic acid spray

ANTISEPTICS *kill germs in order to help mend wounds. Antiseptic sprays were first used in 1865, making surgical operations cleaner and safer than ever before.*

Surgical tools used in the 19th century

In 1886, German surgeon Ernst von Bergmann introduced the technique to STERILIZE SURGICAL INSTRUMENTS AND DRESSINGS *with steam.*

Germ theory

In 1865, Pasteur *investigated* why disease was **destroying silkworm cocoons**. He found **GERMS** were causing the infection. This proved diseases came from harmful types of bacteria and other microorganisms invading living things.

Meister was the first person to receive the rabies vaccine.

By the way...
I always loved to draw and paint in my spare time.

Rabies vaccination

A vaccine is an injection that gives a patient a low dosage of a disease so the ***body recognizes how to fight it effectively***. In 1885, Pasteur created a **VACCINE FOR RABIES** – a deadly disease spread from infected animals to humans. He performed the first rabies vaccination on nine-year-old Joseph Meister. The boy, who had recently been bitten by an infected dog, **recovered fully**.

How he changed the world

Pasteur's pioneering work changed medical science forever. Vaccines have since been developed for many serious diseases that used to be common, saving more than two million lives every year.

Smallpox virus as seen through a microscope

*The vaccine for **SMALLPOX**, originally developed by English scientist Edward Jenner, was so successful that in 1980, the disease was declared extinct.*

Strand of DNA

*In the 1980s, scientists discovered a safer way of making vaccines that didn't involve infection with a virus; they took **DNA** from the disease-causing virus and used it to make a vaccine.*

Dmitri Mendeleev

Chemistry professor who braved the ELEMENTS

The Russian revolutionary behind the ultimate symbol of science – the periodic table of elements.

By the way...
My table was periodic, or repeating, because the properties of the elements I arranged followed a pattern.

St Petersburg University, where Mendeleev taught chemistry

Teacher's textbook

Dmitri Mendeleev was born into a large Russian family in 1834. He studied science before becoming a **chemistry professor** at St Petersburg University in 1867. An entertaining **LECTURER**, he wrote his own chemistry textbook, entitled **The Principles of Chemistry**.

Chemical solitaire

While other scientists were trying to classify the **63 elements known at the time**, Mendeleev is said to have devised a card classification game called **CHEMICAL SOLITAIRE**. He wrote each element's name and symbol on a card and grouped the cards by how heavy each element was. This produced **nine groups of elements that had similar properties.**

Who came before...

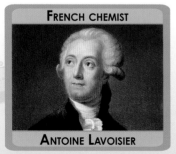

FRENCH CHEMIST

ANTOINE LAVOISIER

The first list of chemical elements was compiled by French chemist **ANTOINE LAVOISIER**, *who also identified and named oxygen in 1778 and hydrogen in 1783.*

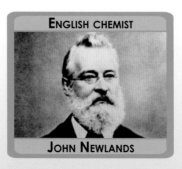

ENGLISH CHEMIST

JOHN NEWLANDS

In 1865, English chemist **JOHN NEWLANDS** *shared his Law of Octaves, according to which every eighth element behaved in a similar way when they were all arranged by the size of their atoms.*

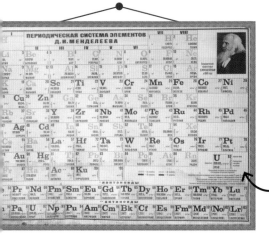

In his element

Grouping the elements by size led Mendeleev to publish the world's first **PERIODIC TABLE OF ELEMENTS** in 1869. Clear and logical patterns could be seen in his arrangement. He even left *empty spaces for undiscovered elements*, which were later proven to be in the right place.

This early version of Mendeleev's periodic table shows the elements that were missing.

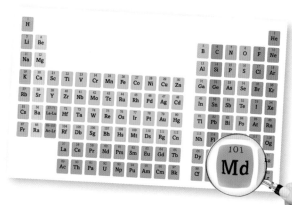

Later life

Mendeleev helped the Russian government build their **first oil refinery** in 1876. A *lifetime believer in liberal causes*, he resigned as professor in 1890 to support a student demonstration against government control. After his death in 1907, Mendeleev's apartment was turned into a museum. In 1955, element 101 was named **MENDELEVIUM** to honour him.

Did you know?

Known for his messy appearance, Mendeleev was said to work too hard to bother with getting his hair cut.

Each element has its own symbol, such as F for fluorine.

How he changed the world

By forming the periodic table, Mendeleev laid the foundations for modern chemistry. This at-a-glance guide to the atomic structures of elements remains the most important tool for scientists and students.

Who came after...

ENGLISH PHYSICIST

HENRY MOSELEY

In 1913, English physicist **HENRY MOSELEY** *discovered a more accurate way to define elements, using their number of protons, rather than the entire mass.*

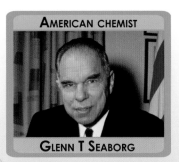

AMERICAN CHEMIST

GLENN T SEABORG

American chemist **GLENN T SEABORG** *was the joint-winner of the Nobel Prize in Chemistry in 1951 for the identification of 10 radioactive elements.*

Inventive chemists

The innovators who created NEW MATERIALS

Scientists are always looking to make stronger, lighter, and longer-lasting materials. Here are some of the greatest success stories.

Charles Goodyear

American engineer Charles Goodyear was the driving force behind **TYRES**. Extreme temperatures cause natural rubber to melt in the heat and freeze in the cold, but Goodyear **heated rubber with a mixture of chemicals to introduce strength and stability**. He patented this process in 1844, making vulcanized (hardened) rubber the *standard for tyres* worldwide.

Tyres are now tougher and harder wearing.

Leo Baekeland

In 1893, Belgian chemist Leo Baekeland created Velox, the **first widely used photographic paper**. This invention was bought by the Kodak camera company, which made Baekeland very rich. He followed this in 1907 with *a light, robust, and malleable plastic*, called **BAKELITE**. Billions of things are now made from bakelite, including components for lighting, jewellery, telephones, and vehicles.

Percy Julian

Known as the soybean chemist, African-American medical researcher Percy Julian applied chemical processes to **soybean plant extracts**. He used the products to create *mass-produced medicines* in the 1940s. His clever synthesis led to various treatments, including one for the eye disease glaucoma. Julian received more than **130 CHEMICAL PATENTS** and gained a number of awards in the process.

Stephanie Kwolek

During her research to develop lightweight, heat-resistant fibres for use in extreme environments, American chemist Stephanie Kwolek discovered **KEVLAR** in 1965. Five times stronger than steel, this sturdy material has **proved a life-saver** as *body armour for the police and military*. Kevlar is also used as a reinforcement material for vehicles and construction.

Bulletproof vests are made from tightly packed Kevlar fibres.

George William Gray

Scottish university professor George William Gray began researching how to make flat television screens in 1970. He found a *molecule called 5CB*, which proved ideal for long-lasting **liquid crystal displays (LCDs)**. His discovery **REVOLUTIONIZED TELEVISIONS**, with 5CB included in 90 per cent of LCDs by the 1980s.

The Curies

The pioneers who explored the science of RADIOACTIVITY

Pierre Curie

Before he met Marie, Pierre Curie **researched crystals and magnetism**. He showed that a substance's **magnetic properties change at a certain temperature**, a level now called the **CURIE POINT**. He joined Marie's radioactive research a few years after they married.

Marie and Pierre Curie, and their daughter Irène, researched radiation, blazing trails in the fields of medicine and nuclear physics.

By the way... My notebooks are radioactive. They're too dangerous to touch and are kept in lead-lined boxes, which trap the radiation.

Marie Curie

Born in Poland, Marie Curie was **taught physics and mathematics** by her father. For further studies, she moved to Paris, France, where she met and married French physicist Pierre Curie. The Curies worked on **RADIOACTIVITY**, and in 1898, they discovered two radioactive elements – **polonium and radium**. For this work, they received the 1903 Nobel Prize in Physics.

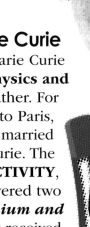

What came after...

In 1928, the GEIGER COUNTER was invented by German physicist Hans Wilhelm Geiger to measure radiation. It produces a "click" when radioactivity is detected.

FOOD IRRADIATION *is the process of exposing food to safe levels of radiation to extend its shelf life. Depending on the dose, the radiation will kill some or all bacteria, moulds, and insects.*

Helping in the war

After Pierre was killed in a road accident in 1906, Marie **continued their radioactivity research** by herself. During World War I, she **developed mobile X-ray units** that could be used near the battlefront. With her teenage daughter Irène, she worked close to the frontline, **X-RAYING INJURED SOLDIERS**.

Marie Curie even drove an ambulance equipped with X-ray apparatus during World War I.

Irène Curie

Marie Curie sparked Irène's **interest in research** when she taught her as a child. Years later, building on her parents' work, Irène Curie and her husband Frédéric Joliot **discovered how to artificially produce radioactive versions of elements**. The pair received the 1935 Nobel Prize in Chemistry. In 1938, she studied the action of neutrons on heavy metals, which led to the discovery of **NUCLEAR FISSION** (the process of splitting apart an atom's nucleus to harness its energy).

Did you know?
Marie Curie is the only woman to win the Nobel Prize twice. She won the Prize in Chemistry in 1911.

How they changed the world

Marie and Pierre's research proved crucial in the use of radium to fight cancer, while Irène's discovery led to great progress in medical treatments and nuclear physics.

Many **SMOKE DETECTORS** contain a radioactive material called americium-241. Smoke particles disrupt the electric current produced by this material, triggering the device's alarm.

NUCLEAR POWER PLANTS use heat generated by nuclear fission to boil water, producing steam. This steam drives giant turbines connected to generators, producing electricity.

Alice Ball

Unsung heroine who saved THOUSANDS OF LIVES

This chemist died too soon and didn't get to see her medical treatment rolled out around the world.

Did you know?
The only chaulmoogra tree at the University of Hawaii features a plaque to commemorate Alice Ball.

The Ball Method

At the University of Hawaii, Ball researched the use of *oil from the chaulmoogra tree in the treatment of leprosy*. This life-threatening condition damages the skin and the nervous system. For centuries, chaulmoogra oil had been applied to skin to treat leprosy, but Ball developed a highly effective, **INJECTABLE FORM OF THE OIL EXTRACT**. This technique of relieving leprosy symptoms came to be known as the **Ball Method**.

Ball investigated the chemical properties of the oil extracted from the seeds of the chaulmoogra berry.

Historic graduation

Alice Augusta Ball was born in Seattle, USA, in 1892. She was *interested in science* at high school and went on to study **PHARMACEUTICAL CHEMISTRY AND PHARMACY** at the University of Washington. In 1915, Ball became **the first woman and the first African-American to** graduate with a master's degree from the University of Hawaii.

What came before...

The **FIRST KNOWN ACCOUNT OF LEPROSY** *is found in an ancient Egyptian papyrus, known as Ebers Papyrus, dating back to about 1550* BCE.

The Ebers Papyrus is one of the oldest records of Egyptian medicine.

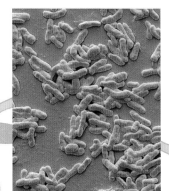

In 1873, **LEPROSY WAS PROVEN TO BE CONTAGIOUS** *when Norwegian doctor Gerhard Henrik Armauer Hansen used a microscope to identify the germ that causes leprosy.*

Ball isolated the necessary chemicals from the oil to develop its injectable form.

Ball being honoured by the University of Hawaii

Belated recognition

Not long after developing the oil extract, Ball died, aged 24. Decades later, in the 21st century, she **received the credit she deserved**. In 2000, the Governor of Hawaii declared 29 February to be **ALICE BALL DAY**, a date celebrated every leap year. The University of Hawaii gave Alice Ball their highest award, the ***Regents' Medal of Distinction***, in 2007.

How she changed the world

Alice Ball's incredible contribution to medicine helped thousands of people and remained the best treatment for leprosy until the 1940s.

Who came after...

In 1947, **MARIE MAYNARD DALY** *became the first African-American to graduate with a PhD in chemistry. She went on to have a successful career in biochemistry.*

Starting in 1979, **DR VIJAY PANNIKAR** *supervised a leprosy therapy using many different anti-bacterial drugs. This greatly reduced leprosy cases.*

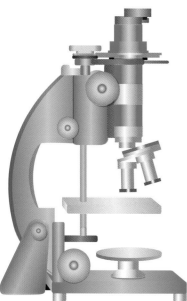

Dorothy Crowfoot Hodgkin

Champ of crystallography who advanced HUMAN HEALTHCARE

This master crystallographer's expert analysis made crystals clear.

Molecular model of vitamin B_{12}

Crystal course

The oldest daughter of an archaeologist and botanist, Hodgkin was born in 1910 in Cairo, Egypt. She **became interested in chemistry and crystals** at the age of 10. After attending school in Suffolk, England, she went to Somerville College at the University of Oxford in 1928 to **study physics and chemistry**. The final year of her course included **CRYSTALLOGRAPHY**, a new field of science examining the arrangement of atoms inside certain solids.

Ilmenite was the first mineral Hodgkin studied as a child.

Structure of penicillin

As a new graduate Hodgkin became an expert in crystallography. In 1942, she was given a sample of **penicillin to analyze**. Penicillin could cure bacterial infections, but its structure remained uncertain. Using X-ray crystallography, Hodgkin studied how X-ray beams diffracted, or bent, in different directions around the atoms in penicillin in order to see **how the atoms were arranged**. She completed the **STRUCTURE OF PENICILLIN** in 1945.

Model of a penicillin molecule

What came before...

In 1822, **TREATISE ON CRYSTALLOGRAPHY**, a book by French mineralogist René-Just Haüy, explained that crystals in minerals can have six different geometrical shapes. This formed the basis of crystallography.

Geometrical shape from *Treatise on Crystallography* by Haüy

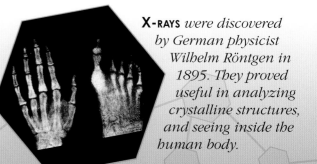

X-RAYS were discovered by German physicist Wilhelm Röntgen in 1895. They proved useful in analyzing crystalline structures, and seeing inside the human body.

Vitamins and insulin

Hodgkin also focused on vitamins – chemicals in food that the body needs to function. Hodgkin's **analysis of the crystal structure of vitamin B$_{12}$,** penicillin and other chemicals won her the Nobel Prize in Chemistry in 1964. She also ***studied insulin***, the hormone that controls the level of sugar in blood. Following three decades of work, her model for insulin was revealed in 1969, which helped in the **TREATMENT OF DIABETES**, a disease that causes high levels of sugar in blood.

Honours list

In 1947, Hodgkin was made a **Fellow of the Royal Society**, the oldest society for science, and the awards kept coming. In 1965, she became the second woman to win the UK's prestigious **ORDER OF MERIT**. She also received the ***Lenin Peace Prize*** and ***the Copley Medal***.

Order of Merit insignia

By the way...

For years my hands made models of molecules I examined. English sculptor Henry Moore did several drawings of my hands in 1978.

How she changed the world

Dorothy Hodgkin pioneered X-ray crystallography techniques, completing structures for penicillin, insulin, and various vitamins, which improved global medicine and healthcare.

The **FIRST X-RAY PHOTOGRAPH OF DIFFRACTION,** *or bending, caused by crystals was produced by German physicist Max von Laue in 1912. He received the Nobel Prize in Physics in 1914 for his work.*

The first **X-RAY SPECTROMETER** *was invented by British physicist William Henry Bragg in 1913. This could be pointed at a crystal from any angle and also determined a diffracted X-ray's intensity.*

Barbara McClintock

The scientist whose JUMPING GENES enabled giant leaps in genetics

This geneticist was the first to suggest that genes can be mobile and reactionary.

Sowing the seeds

Barbara McClintock was born in 1902 in Connecticut, USA, to a doctor father and artist mother. The family moved to New York in 1908 where McClintock attended high school before **enrolling at Cornell University**. A *university course* in 1921 opened her eyes to **BOTANY AND PLANT GENETICS**. She shone academically, earning a bachelor's degree in agriculture, and her master's degree and PhD in botany.

Who came before...

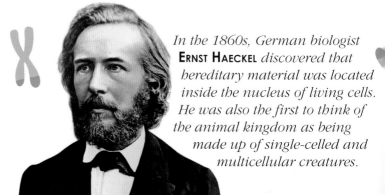

Augustinian monk **GREGOR MENDEL** *studied the genetics of pea plants and realized that peas passed on specific characteristics to later generations. This marked the beginning of the field of heredity genetics.*

In the 1860s, German biologist **ERNST HAECKEL** *discovered that hereditary material was located inside the nucleus of living cells. He was also the first to think of the animal kingdom as being made up of single-celled and multicellular creatures.*

Amazing maize

McClintock's **analysis of the chromosomes of maize**, or corn, revealed *chromosomes* to be the foundation of genetics. For years she studied the colour patterns of maize kernels, making the breakthrough discovery that genetic information changes from one generation to the next. Genetic, or inherited, elements **MOVE WITHIN OR BETWEEN CHROMOSOMES**, producing mutations in the colour and appearance of the maize.

In 1983, McClintock became the first American woman to win an unshared Nobel Prize.

McClintock found genes could change position within a chromosome, known as jumping genes.

She also learned that genes can exchange positions within a pair of chromosomes, known as chromosomal crossover.

Did you know?
About half of the genes in a human can move within or between chromosomes.

Genetics genius

Dismissed as radical, McClintock's work was not accepted by other scientists until the 1960s. **Awards and honours** finally flooded in. McClintock received the **NATIONAL MEDAL OF SCIENCE** in 1970 and a Nobel Prize in 1983. She died in 1992, knowing that her research had played a *pivotal part in the progress of genetics*.

How she changed the world

Barbara McClintock's discoveries changed our understanding of genetics forever. Scientists learned that they could engineer genes, making them perform specific functions to produce desired traits.

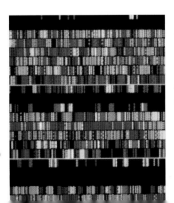

What came after...

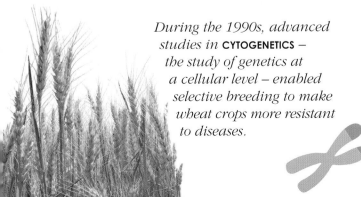

During the 1990s, advanced studies in CYTOGENETICS – the study of genetics at a cellular level – enabled selective breeding to make wheat crops more resistant to diseases.

In 2003, the **HUMAN GENOME PROJECT** was completed. This major international research project revealed the entire sequence of human DNA and mapped the many thousands of human genes.

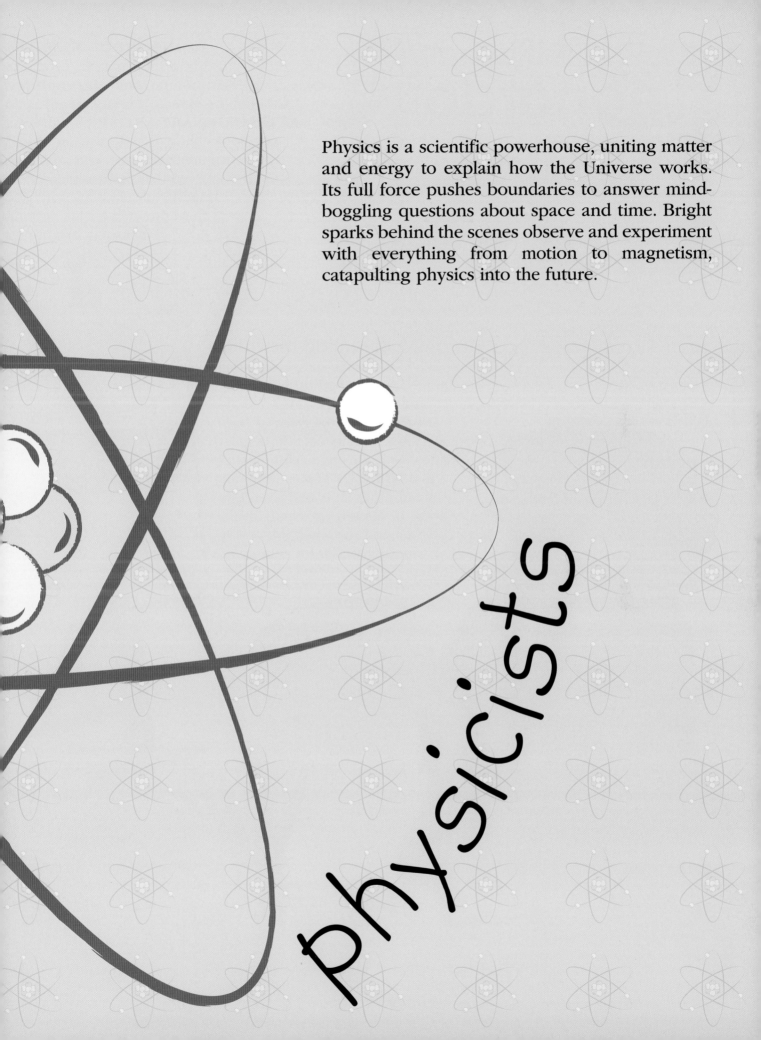

Physics is a scientific powerhouse, uniting matter and energy to explain how the Universe works. Its full force pushes boundaries to answer mind-boggling questions about space and time. Bright sparks behind the scenes observe and experiment with everything from motion to magnetism, catapulting physics into the future.

physicists

Leonardo da Vinci

The GENIUS whose ideas were way ahead of his time

The great observer

Born in Italy in 1452, Leonardo worked as a **painter and engineer**. Although he is mainly remembered as an **EXTRAORDINARY ARTIST**, his surviving notebooks show that he was fascinated by **science, mathematics, and anatomy**. He believed that the world could be explained by observation, and used this approach for his brilliant ideas and inventions.

Inventing the future

Leonardo dissected human bodies, producing **highly accurate anatomical drawings**. He also *studied the properties of light*. His sketchbooks contain detailed designs for futuristic machines, such as a **HELICOPTER** – 500 years ahead of its time. However, few knew of his scientific pursuits at the time and his notebooks went undiscovered for centuries.

This was Leonardo's design for a helicopter, known as an aerial screw.

By the way...
I produced more than 10,000 pages of notes and sketches about my ideas and observations.

How he changed...
Leonardo was one of the world's greatest thinkers and his ideas continue to inspire scientists.

the world

Growing doubts

Nicolaus Copernicus studied astronomy, mathematics, law, and medicine. He worked in an administrative position in a church in Frauenburg, Poland, where he also pursued his interest in **ASTRONOMY**. Copernicus began to **question the established theory** that stated *Earth was stationary at the centre of the Universe* with the Moon, Sun, and planets moving around it in circular paths.

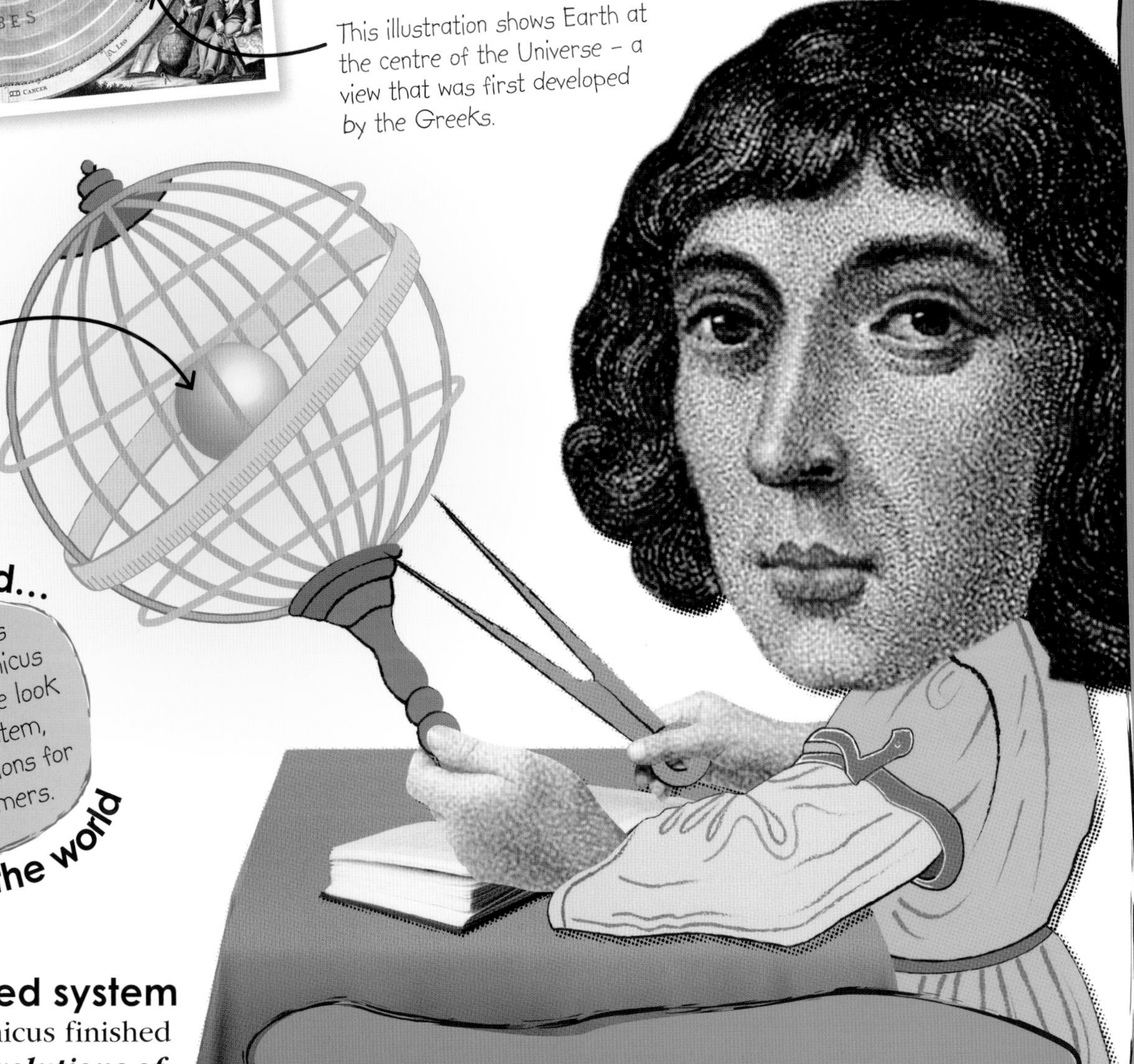

This illustration shows Earth at the centre of the Universe – a view that was first developed by the Greeks.

Copernicus put the Sun in the middle of his model of the Universe.

How he changed...

Through countless calculations, Copernicus changed the way we look at the Solar System, laying the foundations for future astronomers.

the world

Sun-centred system

By 1530, Copernicus finished his book, *The Revolutions of the Celestial Spheres*. His main theory was that **the planets – including Earth – revolved around the Sun.** Copernicus was **CORRECT**, but because this contradicted the church's belief that Earth was at the centre of the Universe, he did not release his book until a few months before his death.

Nicolaus Copernicus

The astronomer who REWROTE the rules of the Universe by placing the Sun at its centre

Galileo Galilei

STARRY-EYED scientist

By the way...
I was the first person to use a telescope to look at the Solar System and record my observations.

The sky was the limit for this multi-talented astronomer, inventor, mathematician, and physicist whose ideas have stood the test of time.

Galileo taught Mathematics at the University of Padua, Italy.

Distant dream

Born in 1564 near Pisa, Italy, Galileo Galilei studied **MATHEMATICS** before becoming a professor in 1589. He made many discoveries and designs throughout his life. When Galileo learned of an *invention called a telescope* in 1609, he decided to **create his own version**.

Who came before...

An inspiration for Galileo, Greek scientist **ARCHIMEDES** *was among the first to claim that Earth orbits the Sun. He also used mathematics rather than logic to solve problems.*

Persian philosopher and scientist **AVICENNA** *was the first to record that moving objects can be slowed down by external factors.*

78

Over the Moon

Originally intended to **WATCH ENEMY SHIPS AT SEA**, Galileo's telescope made **objects appear so much larger** that he turned his eyes to the skies. This long-distance visual aid revealed *mountains and valleys on the Moon, spots on the Sun, and moons orbiting the planet Jupiter*.

Central Sun

Up until the 16th century, most people believed Earth was the *fixed centre of the Universe*, orbited by the Sun and planets. Galileo witnessed the planets Mercury and Venus **CIRCLING THE SUN**, and put forward the controversial idea that **Earth also orbits the Sun**. This supported Nicolaus Copernicus's view of the Universe, but went against beliefs of the time. The Church put Galileo under house arrest.

The planets revolve around the Sun as Copernicus claimed.

Physics in Pisa

Galileo carried out many experiments in Pisa. According to some accounts, he threw **two cannonballs** of different weights from the *Leaning Tower* to show that falling objects of different weights land at the **SAME TIME**. This proved that heavy and light objects fall at the same speed, assisted by gravity.

How he changed the world

By combining logic with his experiments and observations, Galileo established new laws of physics and changed the way people viewed the Solar System.

Who came after...

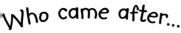

In 1687, English scientist **ISAAC NEWTON** published his book Principia, *which developed Galileo's theory that different objects fall at the same speed.*

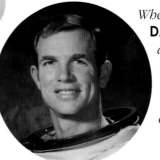

When American astronaut **DAVE SCOTT** *dropped a hammer and a feather on the Moon in 1971, they landed at the same time, proving that all objects fall at the same speed even on the lunar surface.*

Johannes Kepler

An astronomer who revealed how the PLANETS ORBIT the Sun

Copernicus's model, with the Sun at the centre of the Universe

Planetary puzzle

German astronomer Johannes Kepler initially agreed with Copernicus's theory that the **Sun is at the centre** of the Universe, with the planets orbiting it in **CIRCULAR PATHS**. However, this did not explain the *movements* of the planets as seen from Earth.

How he changed...

Kepler's ideas greatly influenced later scientists – Isaac Newton used Kepler's laws when developing his ideas about gravity.

the world

Kepler's model of the Solar System supported Copernicus's theory.

Redrawing the Universe

Kepler worked closely with leading Danish astronomer **Tycho Brahe**. Using Brahe's data, Kepler **CALCULATED** that each planet moves around the Sun in an oval path, known as an elliptical orbit. He also observed that planets' speeds vary according to their distances from the Sun. These ideas formed the basis of his *laws of planetary movement*.

Stargazer

Christiaan Huygens was born into a wealthy Dutch family in 1629. Fascinated by astronomy, he constructed his own *powerful telescope* and discovered one of Saturn's moons – later called **TITAN**. Huygens also realized that what Galileo had described as "ears" on the side of Saturn were actually **rings circling the planet**.

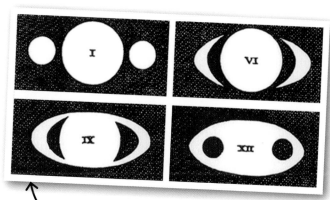

Drawings of Saturn from Huygens's *Systema Saturnium*

Huygens improved the accuracy of his pendulum clock.

Christiaan Huygens

The multitalented scientist who made DISCOVERIES in many areas of science

How he changed...

Although future experiments showed that Huygens's light theory wasn't correct, his work established the idea that light is a wave.

the world

Making waves

In 1657, Huygens designed a clock with a **PENDULUM**, vastly improving accuracy by reducing the loss of time from 15 minutes a day to just 15 seconds. However, he is perhaps best known for his **theory of light**, published in 1690. In contrast to the theory that light is composed of particles, Huygens proposed that *light travels in waves* through a substance called ether. This theory enabled him to explain both reflection and refraction (bending) of light.

Star tales

Edmond Halley was born in 1656. While studying at the University of Oxford, he became interested in **ASTRONOMY**. He left university early to travel to the South Atlantic where he documented the **celestial position of 341 stars**. He later *met Isaac Newton* and helped him to publish his groundbreaking theories about gravity.

Halley catalogued lots of stars, including a cluster in the Centaurus constellation.

Halley's Comet is the only comet visible to the naked eye, and might appear twice in a person's lifetime.

Halley's Comet

In 1705, Halley made his most famous discovery. He noticed that descriptions of *comets sighted in 1531, 1607, and 1682 were very similar*. He eventually realized that these sightings were actually all of the same comet that came near to Earth roughly **every 76 years**. He correctly **PREDICTED** that it would return in 1758, but sadly died before seeing his prediction come true.

How he changed...

Halley's calculations proved that comets revolve around the Sun. His work also confirmed that Newton's laws of gravity are applicable to all celestial bodies.

the world

Edmond Halley

The scientist who predicted the reappearance of the world's MOST FAMOUS COMET

Halley's famous book describes the orbits of 24 comets.

A SYNOPSIS OF THE ASTRONOMY OF COMETS

By EDMUND HALLEY, Savilian Professor of Geometry at Oxford; And Fellow of the Royal Society.

Translated from the ORIGINAL, printed at Oxford.

LONDON
Printed for John Senex, next to the Fleece Tavern, in Cornhill. 1705.

Leavitt studied photographic plates of the night sky to determine the position and brightness of stars.

How she changed...

Leavitt's discovery led to an understanding of the Universe's vast scale and allowed distances of the stars to be measured from Earth.

the world

Star snapshots

Born in 1868, Henrietta Leavitt studied astronomy before joining the Harvard College Observatory, USA. She analyzed photographs of the night sky, **recording how bright each star was**. In particular, she studied **VARIABLE STARS** – stars that vary in brightness. Leavitt calculated *how long it took these stars to complete a cycle* from brightness to dimness and back to brightness again.

Henrietta Swan Leavitt

The unsung astronomer whose work on stars led to a way of MEASURING the Universe

Stellar discovery

Focusing on a class of variable stars called **CEPHEIDS**, Leavitt noticed there was a direct *relationship between the time it takes for a star to complete a cycle and how bright that star is*. This is known as the **period-luminosity relation**. Using this rule to work out how bright a star is, scientists were able to calculate the distance of these stars from Earth.

The length of a Cepheid's cycle predicts how bright it is.

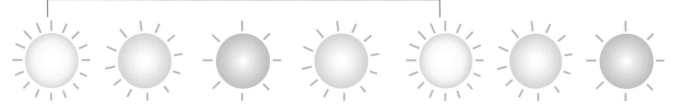

Isaac Newton's description of the forces that govern the Universe made him one of the most influential scientists of all time.

Isaac Newton

The GENIUS who laid down the laws of gravity and motion

Newton conducted many experiments at his home, Woolsthorpe Manor in Lincolnshire.

Early beginnings

Born in England in 1643, Isaac Newton had a lonely childhood. His mother wanted him to become a farmer, but Newton was more *interested in designing devices* such as sundials and clocks. In 1661, he began studying at the **University of Cambridge**. During the **GREAT PLAGUE**, the university was closed, and Newton was forced to return home.

Did you know?
Newton believed that experimentation was more important than reading books.

Who came before...

In 1543, Polish astronomer **NICOLAUS COPERNICUS** published his book in which he argued that the Sun, and not Earth, was the centre of the Solar System.

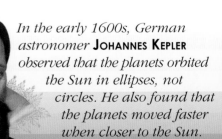

In the early 1600s, German astronomer **JOHANNES KEPLER** observed that the planets orbited the Sun in ellipses, not circles. He also found that the planets moved faster when closer to the Sun.

Invisible force

Newton's time at home was productive. When he saw an **APPLE** fall from a tree, he started thinking about the force that brought it down. He developed his *theory of gravity* – which explains **why objects fall to Earth and why Earth orbits the Sun**.

PHILOSOPHIÆ
NATURALIS
PRINCIPIA
MATHEMATICA·

Autore JS. NEWTON, Trin. Coll. Cantab. Soc. Mathefeos Profeffore Lucafiano, & Societatis Regalis Sodali.

IMPRIMATUR·
S. PEPYS, Reg. Soc. PRÆSES.
Julii 5. 1686;

LONDINI,
Juffu Societatis Regiæ ac Typis Jofephi Streater. Proftant Venales apud Sam. Smith ad infignia Principis Walliæ in Cœmiterio D. Pauli, aliofq; nonnullos Bibliopolas. Anno MDCLXXXVII.

Revolutionary book

In 1687, Newton published *Principia Mathematica*, which set out his **THREE LAWS OF MOTION**. These explained what makes an object move or stop; what makes it move faster or slower, or change direction; and how *for every action there is an equal and opposite reaction.*

Newton's reflecting telescope

By the way...
I was a keen alchemist, and spent years experimenting in my quest for the mythical philosopher's stone, believed to turn metal to gold.

Flashes of brilliance

Newton developed a type of mathematics called **CALCULUS**. He was also the first to prove that **light is composed of different colours** when he passed sunlight through a prism (a triangular glass block). In 1668, he designed a powerful *reflecting telescope* that used mirrors instead of lenses.

How he changed the world

Newton's work transformed science. He introduced the concept of gravity and explained the forces that make the Universe work.

Who came after...

French physicist **ÉMILIE DU CHÂTELET** *worked on the translation of Newton's work* Principia Mathematica, *and tested his theories during the 1740s.*

German physicist **ALBERT EINSTEIN** *published his general theory of relativity in 1916. His theories changed people's understanding of time, space, matter, and energy.*

James Clerk Maxwell

This giant of physics revolutionized science when he united the fields of electricity and magnetism in one theory.

The Scottish physicist who created the theory of ELECTROMAGNETISM, paving the way for radio and television

Maxwell showed that both magnetism and electricity are forms of electromagnetic fields.

In the 1980s, Maxwell's theory about Saturn's rings was proved correct by the *Voyager* spacecraft.

Inquisitive mind

Curious as a child, James Clerk Maxwell published his *first scientific paper at the age of 14*. In 1856, he published a major **ESSAY ON SATURN'S RINGS**. Scientists had long struggled to understand why they didn't break up or move apart. Using mathematics, Maxwell suggested they were neither entirely solid nor a fluid, but made up of lots of separate parts.

Maxwell's equations

Maxwell's most famous discovery was that *electricity and magnetism are essentially two aspects of the same force*. He also showed that electric and magnetic fields travel through space in the form of waves, and that **light is a type of electromagnetic wave**. His **FOUR MATHEMATICAL EQUATIONS**, which describe the behaviour of electric and magnetic fields and how they interact with matter, are considered a cornerstone of modern physics.

Did you know?
Albert Einstein was inspired by Maxwell and had a photograph of him on his study wall.

Who came before...

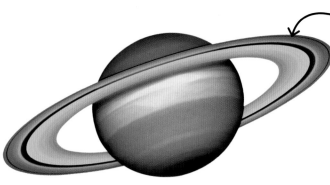

A link between electricity and magnetism was found in 1820 by Danish physicist **HANS CHRISTIAN OERSTED,** *who showed that electricity flowing through a wire could move a nearby magnet.*

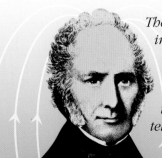

The electromagnet was invented in 1825 by English electrical engineer **WILLIAM STURGEON**. *This led to the development of the telegraph in the 1830s, the first step in electric telecommunications.*

Colour photography was born with Maxwell's image of a tartan ribbon.

By the way...
As my classmates didn't understand my genius, they nicknamed me "Dafty".

Colourful career

Maxwell made many important **advances in understanding colour perception** and colour blindness, and produced the **WORLD'S FIRST COLOUR PHOTOGRAPH** in 1861. He carried out pioneering *research into the speed of molecules in a gas* at different temperatures. Maxwell also designed and then led the Cavendish Laboratory – the renowned physics department at the University of Cambridge.

How he changed the world

Maxwell's equations laid the groundwork for Einstein's special theory of relativity and led to the development of technology such as radio, television, and mobile phones.

What came after...

The **FIRST PRACTICAL RADIO TRANSMITTER AND RECEIVER** *was developed by Italian inventor Guglielmo Marconi in the mid-1890s. He sent the first long-distance wireless transmission across the Atlantic Ocean in 1901.*

Engineers use Maxwell's equations to create modern technology. The high-speed **MAGLEV TRAINS** *for example, "float" above the track using a magnet that repels another magnet on the track.*

Ernest Rutherford

The physicist who ushered in the ATOMIC AGE

This super scientist worked out what's at the heart of atoms and established a new science – nuclear physics.

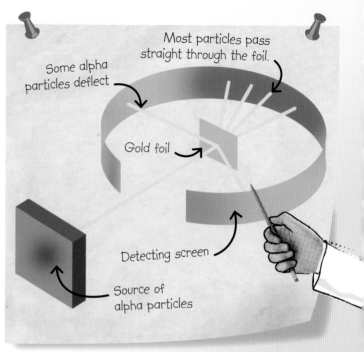

Most particles pass straight through the foil.

Some alpha particles deflect

Gold foil

Detecting screen

Source of alpha particles

Rutherford's research laboratory at the University of Cambridge, England

Golden discovery

In 1909, Rutherford and his researchers conducted an important experiment. **Positively charged particles called alpha rays** were fired at a very thin gold foil. Although most particles passed straight through, some were deflected. This proved that atoms are mostly empty space with a tiny, positively charged centre – the **NUCLEUS**. Rutherford likened his *new model of the atom* to that of the Solar System with the nucleus in the centre and electrons orbiting around it.

Nobel Prize

Talented scientist Ernest Rutherford was born in New Zealand in 1871. He discovered that *atoms of some elements break down into lighter atoms*, giving off a kind of energy called **RADIOACTIVITY**. In 1908, **Rutherford won the Nobel Prize in Chemistry** for his discovery.

Did you know?
During World War I, Rutherford performed secret experiments to find ways of detecting German U-boats.

Who came before...

Chemist **JOHN DALTON** built on the theories that had existed since ancient Greek times. In the 1800s, he concluded that all chemical elements are composed of indestructible atoms.

In 1897, physicist **J J THOMPSON** discovered the electron – the negatively charged particle of an atom. He was awarded the Nobel Prize in Physics in 1906.

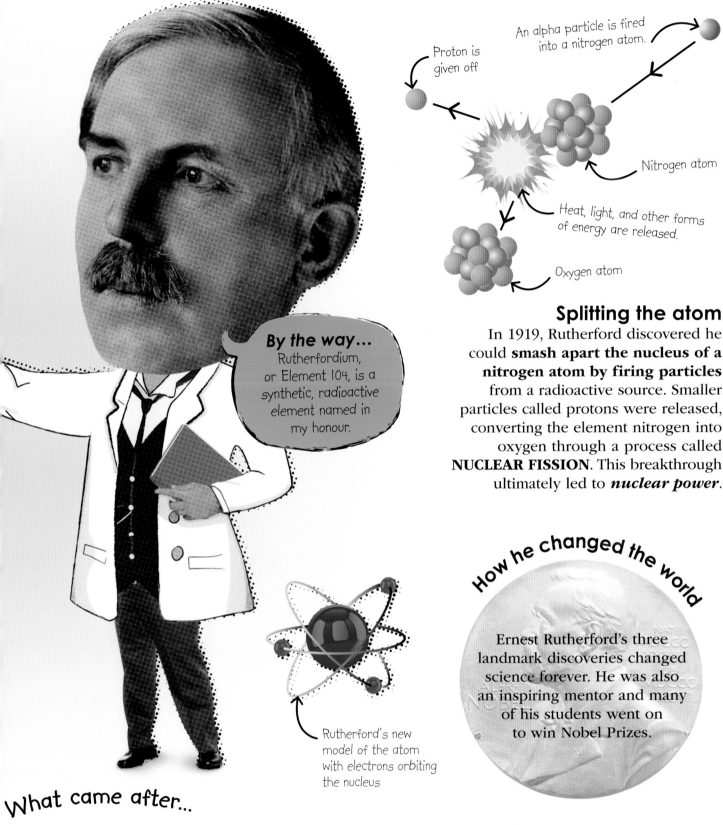

An alpha particle is fired into a nitrogen atom.

Proton is given off

Nitrogen atom

Heat, light, and other forms of energy are released.

Oxygen atom

Splitting the atom

In 1919, Rutherford discovered he could **smash apart the nucleus of a nitrogen atom by firing particles** from a radioactive source. Smaller particles called protons were released, converting the element nitrogen into oxygen through a process called **NUCLEAR FISSION**. This breakthrough ultimately led to *nuclear power*.

By the way...
Rutherfordium, or Element 104, is a synthetic, radioactive element named in my honour.

Rutherford's new model of the atom with electrons orbiting the nucleus

How he changed the world

Ernest Rutherford's three landmark discoveries changed science forever. He was also an inspiring mentor and many of his students went on to win Nobel Prizes.

What came after...

In 1932, James Chadwick used this detector to identify **NEUTRONS** *(particles that have no electric charge) in an atom's nucleus. Neutrons help hold the nucleus together.*

In 2012, a subatomic particle called the **HIGGS BOSON** *was detected by the Large Hadron Collider, a machine that smashes atoms together at almost the speed of light.*

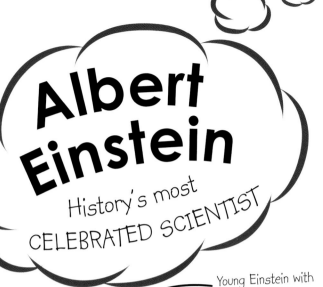

Albert Einstein

History's most CELEBRATED SCIENTIST

This prize-winning physicist's groundbreaking theories about the Universe transformed modern thinking.

Young Einstein with his sister, Maja

By the way...
My fascination with physics began with a magnetic compass I was given as a boy.

Growing genius
Born in Ulm, Germany, in 1879, Albert Einstein was slow to speak and talked in whispers. After finishing school, he started an **office job** in Switzerland and filled his spare time by **WRITING** scientific *theories about space, time, and motion*.

Who came before...

In 1881, Polish physics teacher **ALBERT A MICHELSON** *measured the speed of light with the greatest accuracy at that time. This data helped form Einstein's theory of relativity.*

German theoretical physicist **MAX PLANCK** *was the first to put forward quantum theory, which explained atomic and subatomic processes. This won him the Nobel Prize in Physics in 1918.*

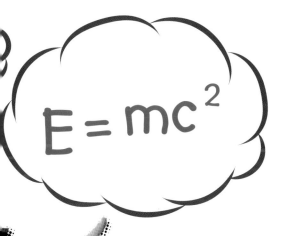

$$E = mc^2$$

The theory

The 1905 publication of Einstein's **theory of special relativity** showed that space and time are linked and can change. A decade later, he expanded this theory to include **GRAVITY** and named it the **theory of general relativity.** By now, Einstein believed that space and time were one thing, called *spacetime*.

Einstein's original paper on the theory of special and general relativity was first published in German.

The Nobel prize ceremony in Stockholm, Sweden

Famous formula

Einstein is best known for his equation **E = mc²**, which is used to calculate **ENERGY**. E is for energy, m is mass, and c is the speed of light (299,792 km/s or 186,282 miles/s). The formula shows that *even a tiny amount of matter can have a massive amount of energy*. This helped physicists understand that they could harness a lot of energy from atoms.

How he changed the world

Einstein was elevated to superstar status when his scientific equations and theories of relativity were proven correct, advancing modern physics forever.

Ahead of his time

Einstein received the **NOBEL PRIZE** in Physics in 1921, and travelled the world giving *lectures*. After his death in 1955, his brain was donated to research. The autopsy revealed that his brain was smaller than average, but the area for **mathematical reasoning** was larger.

What came after...

Einstein's famous equation E = mc² was proved when the first NUCLEAR BOMB exploded in 1945. The energy inside atoms was released in huge nuclear reactions.

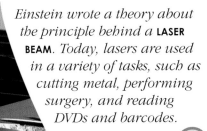

Einstein wrote a theory about the principle behind a LASER BEAM. Today, lasers are used in a variety of tasks, such as cutting metal, performing surgery, and reading DVDs and barcodes.

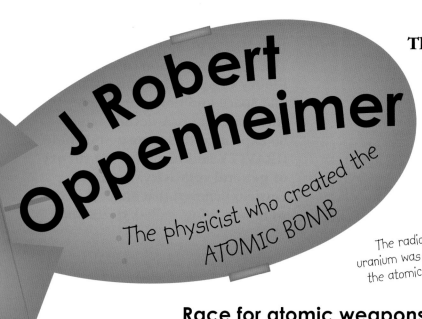

J Robert Oppenheimer

The physicist who created the ATOMIC BOMB

This brilliant American scientist made many important contributions, but he is known for developing the devastating nuclear bombs that ended World War II.

The radioactive element uranium was used as fuel in the atomic bombs in 1945.

Race for atomic weapons

Born in 1904, Oppenheimer went to Harvard University, USA, where he became immersed in the world of atoms and how they interact with each other. During World War II, the Allies feared that Nazi Germany would build an **ATOMIC BOMB**, so in 1942, Oppenheimer was **appointed** the director of the *Manhattan Project*, the Allied effort to develop atomic weapons first.

The Trinity test

Oppenheimer established the **Los Alamos National Laboratory** in New Mexico and recruited a team of leading scientists. In July 1945, a plutonium bomb was successfully detonated at a remote test site in nearby Alamogordo. Code-named *Trinity*, this test created a crater over 300 m (980 ft) wide and ushered in the **ATOMIC AGE**.

Replicas of the two atomic bombs, Little Boy (left) and Fat Man

An atomic bomb explodes into a mushroom cloud.

Did you know?
Oppenheimer was nominated for the Nobel Prize in Physics three times, in 1945, 1951, and 1967, but never won.

Who came before...

In the 1930s, Austrian physicist **Lise Meitner** *and German chemist* **Otto Hahn** *discovered nuclear fission – nuclear technology relies on this process – when they split a uranium nucleus by bombarding it with neutrons.*

Italian physicist **Enrico Fermi** *developed the first nuclear chain reaction in 1942. This is the process in which a neutron splits a uranium atom, producing more neutrons that split further uranium atoms.*

Genbaku Dome, the only building to survive the attack on Hiroshima, Japan

Nuclear age

Shortly after the Trinity test, two *atomic bombs* were dropped on Japan, swiftly ending **World War II**. Filled with remorse, Oppenheimer went on to argue against the development of a deadlier hydrogen bomb. He was initially accused of disloyalty, but in 1963 was awarded the **ENRICO FERMI AWARD** for his contribution to physics.

By the way...
After the first atomic bomb destroyed Hiroshima in Japan, I voiced my regret with words from the *Bhagavad Gita*, "Now I am become Death, the destroyer of worlds."

How he changed the world

The development of nuclear weaponry, with its potential for mass destruction, has been seen both as a supreme scientific achievement and a disaster for the modern world.

Who came after...

Hungarian-born physicist **EDWARD TELLER** led the development of the more powerful hydrogen bomb. This bomb relies on atomic nuclei fusing together, rather than atoms splitting apart, to produce explosive energy.

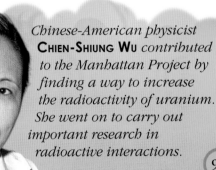

Chinese-American physicist **CHIEN-SHIUNG WU** contributed to the Manhattan Project by finding a way to increase the radioactivity of uranium. She went on to carry out important research in radioactive interactions.

Penzias and Wilson

This lucky duo accidentally discovered cosmic microwave background (CMB) radiation – the leftover heat from the Big Bang, the Universe's fiery origin.

The astronomers who heard the echo of the Universe's EXPLOSIVE BIRTH

The Holmdel Horn Antenna picked up a mysterious background noise, which came from space wherever the device was pointed.

Static in space

Arno Penzias met Robert Woodrow Wilson at **BELL LABORATORIES** in New Jersey, USA, where they worked as radio astronomers (astronomers looking for radio waves from space). In 1965, they were using a *giant horn antenna to detect microwave radiation* – an invisible form of light – from space. When they turned it to the edge of the Milky Way, they were puzzled to hear a **strange background noise** that sounded like radio static.

Who came before...

In 1917, Dutch astronomer **WILLEM DE SITTER** *applied Einstein's general theory of relativity to his study of space, and proposed a Universe that was curved and constantly expanding.*

In 1931, French priest and astronomer **GEORGES LEMAÎTRE** *suggested that the Universe expanded from a single particle called the Primeval Atom – an event that we now call the Big Bang.*

Accidental discovery

Almost at the same time Penzias and Wilson made their discovery, physicist Robert Dicke predicted that if the **BIG BANG** – the theory that the Universe began from a big explosion – had indeed occurred, then *trace amounts of leftover heat radiation would exist* throughout the Universe. When Penzias and Wilson heard of his prediction, **they realized the significance of their discovery**.

The Big Bang produced an incredible amount of heat energy, traces of which can still be detected as microwave radiation.

Map of CMB created from data gathered by a space probe

The red parts are the hottest and the blue parts are the coldest.

Legacy

The radiation was interpreted as CMB, and was the **first real evidence of the Big Bang**. Space probes have now gathered **MORE DATA ABOUT CMB**, which has helped scientists make *key observations about the Universe*, including estimating its age and trying to understand how its structure was formed.

By the way...
After ruling out radio noise from nearby cities, we thought the static sound was caused by bird droppings in the antenna.

How they changed the world

Penzias and Wilson's Nobel Prize-winning discovery transformed our understanding of space, allowing astronomers to study the age of the Universe, its shape, and composition.

What came after...

In 1989, the **COSMIC BACKGROUND EXPLORER (COBE) SATELLITE** *was launched. It studied CMB and its findings provided important evidence to support the Big Bang theory.*

From 2009 to 2013, the **PLANCK SPACECRAFT** *studied CMB in greater detail than ever before. The resulting map suggested that the Universe came into existence 13.82 billion years ago.*

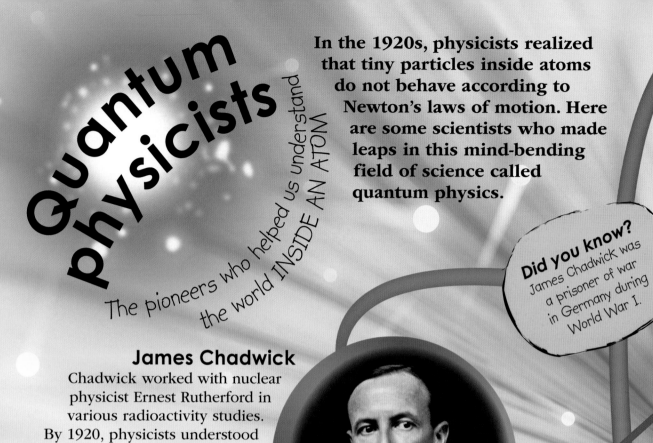

Quantum physicists

The pioneers who helped us understand the world INSIDE AN ATOM

In the 1920s, physicists realized that tiny particles inside atoms do not behave according to Newton's laws of motion. Here are some scientists who made leaps in this mind-bending field of science called quantum physics.

Did you know?
James Chadwick was a prisoner of war in Germany during World War I.

James Chadwick

Chadwick worked with nuclear physicist Ernest Rutherford in various radioactivity studies. By 1920, physicists understood that **most of an atom's mass lay in its central nucleus**, which contained protons (particles with a positive electric charge). In 1932, Chadwick confirmed that an atom's nucleus *also contained uncharged particles*, which he named **NEUTRONS**. This discovery won him the 1935 Nobel Prize in Physics.

Werner Heisenberg

Awarded the Nobel Prize in Physics in 1932, this German-born physicist is best known for developing the **UNCERTAINTY PRINCIPLE**. This tells us that unlike Newton's Universe – in which things run according to firm laws – there is only so much we can know **about how tiny particles behave** inside atoms. You can know where a particle is, or how fast it is moving, but can't know both things. Their *random behaviour can only be predicted on the basis of probability*.

Subrahmanyan Chandrasekhar

This Nobel Prize-winning Indian-American astrophysicist is best known for his proof that there is an **upper limit to the mass of a white dwarf star**. Using principles of quantum physics, he showed that **ANY STAR EXCEEDING THE CHANDRASEKHAR LIMIT** (a mass equalling 1.4 times the mass of the Sun) will end its life as a supernova – *a violently exploding star*.

Richard Feynman

American physicist Richard Feynman was awarded the Nobel Prize in Physics in 1965 for his contributions to the development of *quantum electrodynamics* (the theory of the interaction of light and matter). He created **FEYNMAN DIAGRAMS** – graphics of interactions between the tiny particles inside atoms. He was also a key figure in the top-secret **Manhattan Project,** which created the atomic bomb.

Peter Higgs

In 1964, this English theoretical physicist predicted the existence of *an invisible field that gives mass to every single object in the Universe*. Many scientists disagreed with the idea, but 48 years later, the Large Hadron Collider (a powerful particle smasher in Geneva) confirmed the existence of the **HIGGS BOSON**, a **particle associated with this field**, which proved his theory. Higgs received the Nobel Prize in Physics in 2013.

Did you know?
Stephen Hawking bet another scientist $100 that the Higgs boson would never be discovered.

97

Edwin Hubble

The astronomer whose studies of DISTANT GALAXIES expanded our understanding of the Universe

Hubble proved that we live in a Universe of billions of galaxies, and that it is rapidly expanding.

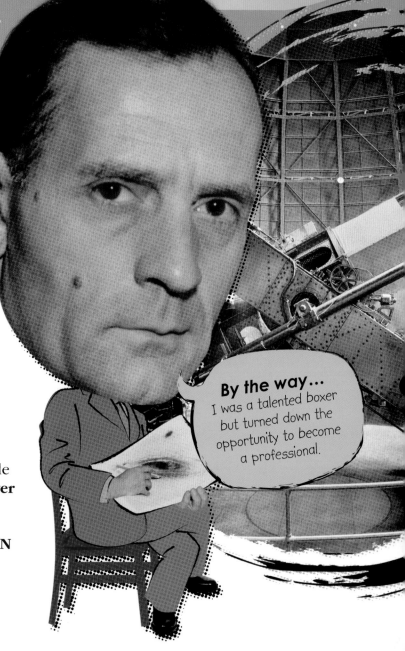

By the way...
I was a talented boxer but turned down the opportunity to become a professional.

Change of direction

Born in Missouri, USA, in 1889, Edwin Hubble was a **high school teacher and then a lawyer before turning to astronomy**. After gaining a PhD, he *served in World War I* and then started a research job at the **MOUNT WILSON OBSERVATORY** in California in 1919.

Who came before...

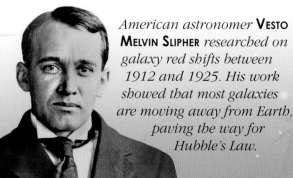

In 1750, English astronomer **THOMAS WRIGHT** *was the first to describe the shape of the Milky Way. He speculated that faint cloudy spots, or nebulae, could be distant galaxies.*

American astronomer **VESTO MELVIN SLIPHER** *researched on galaxy red shifts between 1912 and 1925. His work showed that most galaxies are moving away from Earth, paving the way for Hubble's Law.*

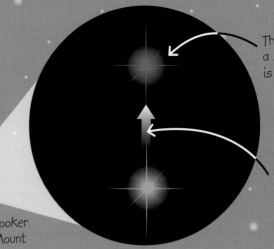

The red shift effect is a sign that a star is moving away from us.

As a star moves further away, its light appears redder.

Hubble used the Hooker Telescope at the Mount Wilson Observatory.

Beyond the Milky Way

At the time, astronomers believed the Milky Way made up the entire Universe. However, while *studying a cluster of stars*, Hubble identified a **CEPHEID VARIABLE** – a giant star that gets brighter and dimmer with time. Using Henrietta Swan Leavitt's period-luminosity relation, he **worked out that this star was actually about a million light years away** and part of an entirely separate galaxy to our own.

A Cepheid variable glows brighter than the stars around it.

Hubble's Law

As a light source moves away from an observer, the wavelengths of light are stretched, producing red light. Astronomers noted this **RED SHIFT EFFECT** in the wavelengths of distant stars – a sign that these stars and their galaxies are moving away from Earth. Hubble realized that **the more distant a galaxy, the greater its speed**. Known as Hubble's Law, this provided the *first proof that the Universe is expanding*.

How he changed the world

Hubble's discovery that there are galaxies outside our own profoundly changed our view of the Universe. His research led to the realization that space is expanding and laid the groundwork for the Big Bang theory.

What came after...

The **HUBBLE CONSTANT** *is the measurement unit that describes the Universe's expansion. American astronomer Allan Sandage played a key role in determining it.*

Launched in 1990, the **HUBBLE SPACE TELESCOPE** *orbits Earth every 97 minutes. Beaming back images of distant galaxies, it has peered at regions 13.4 billion light years away.*

Vera Rubin

The dark matter detective who proved that most of the Universe is INVISIBLE

Rubin found evidence of the mysterious dark matter that affects how stars move within galaxies.

Did you know?
In 1965, Rubin became the first woman to use the powerful telescopes at the Palomar Observatory, California, USA, for her research.

Young astronomer

Vera Rubin was born in Pennsylvania, USA, in 1928. **Fascinated by the night sky** from an early age, she built her own *telescope out of cardboard* at the age of 14. Determined to pursue her passion, she studied **ASTRONOMY** – despite being told that it was an unsuitable career for a woman.

Puzzling discovery

Rubin studied spiral galaxies and discovered that their **outer stars moved much faster** than expected. Since most of a **GALAXY'S MASS** lies at its centre, she had expected the outer stars to move more slowly than the inner ones – just as the outer planets in our Solar System *orbit the Sun more slowly* than the inner planets. This is because the pull of gravity weakens with distance.

Who came before...

In 1932, Dutch astronomer **JAN HENDRIK OORT** suggested the existence of invisible matter after discovering that the mass of the Milky Way must be greater than what could be detected visually.

In 1934, Swiss astronomer **FRITZ ZWICKY** discovered that the speed of galaxies in the Coma Cluster was faster than predicted. He concluded there must be matter that could not be seen, and called it dark matter.

Rubin studied the Andromeda galaxy in particular because of how close it is to Earth.

By the way...
When asked about my discovery on dark matter, I said, "I'm sorry we all know so little. But that's kind of the fun, isn't it?"

Mysterious matter

Rubin's calculations showed that these galaxies must contain a heavy, but invisible, ingredient – known as **DARK MATTER** – that holds them together. After further research, she concluded that spiral galaxies contain around 10 times *more dark matter* than visible matter – and therefore that most of the mass of the Universe is **hidden from view**.

How she changed the world

Rubin's discovery transformed astronomy, and while scientists still don't know what dark matter is, they believe it accounts for about 95 per cent of the Universe, along with a mysterious force called dark energy.

Rubin used a spectrometer to view previously invisible starlight.

Who came after...

American astronomer **W KENT FORD** *worked closely with Rubin on her dark matter theory. He developed an extremely sensitive spectrometer – an instrument that detects invisible light – for the research.*

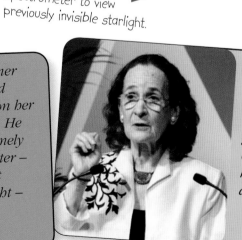

Today, **NETA A BAHCALL**, *a prominent astrophysicist and professor, investigates the formation of galaxies, the structure of the Universe, and how dark matter is distributed within it.*

Stephen Hawking

The most famous ASTROPHYSICIST in the Universe

Exemplifying the triumph of mind over matter, this scientist redefined black holes.

Overcoming obstacles

Born in Oxford, England, growing up Hawking *enjoyed science and stargazing*. He graduated in Natural Science from the University of Oxford in 1962, and went to Cambridge for his PhD in Cosmology. In 1963, he was **diagnosed with motor neurone disease**, which affected his nerve cells. Given just two years to live, Hawking would go on to **DEFY THE ODDS**.

Stephen Hawking

By the way... I have guest-starred in many popular television shows such as *The Simpsons* and *The Big Bang Theory*.

Hawking radiation

Many physicists, including Einstein, suggested the idea of the existence of a **black hole** – a small point with high density created by the collapse of a heavy star. When Hawking researched black holes, he found that they could produce radiation in the form of tiny particles. Called **HAWKING RADIATION**, it disproved the scientific belief that nothing can escape the pull of a black hole's gravity. He theorized that if a black hole gives off this radiation without taking in other matter, it *will eventually fade away*.

Who came before...

England's **JOHN MICHELL** *and France's* **PIERRE-SIMON LAPLACE** *were the first to theorize the black hole as an invisible star during the late 1700s.*

Pierre-Simon Laplace

The work of German theoretical physicist **ALBERT EINSTEIN** *– especially the relationship between space, time, and gravity – remains the biggest influence on Stephen Hawking.*

Matter from a star is pulled into a black hole.

Event horizon is the point of no return – anything that crosses this boundary can never escape the pull of the black hole's gravity.

Books in brief

Hawking published his first book, *The Large Scale Structure of Space-Time*, in 1973, but it was *A Brief History of Time*, published in 1988, that **made Hawking a celebrity**. This book explained the Big Bang and black holes for the everyday reader. It became the **MOST POPULAR SCIENCE BOOK OF ALL TIME**.

Named after the astrophysicist himself, The Stephen Hawking Medal For Science Communication was launched in 2015.

Final frontier

Despite his illness, **Hawking refuses to limit his life or work**. He travels internationally giving lectures on astrophysics. In 2007, he *experienced weightlessness* on a modified aircraft at the Kennedy Space Centre in Florida, USA. Hawking's **HONOURS** include the Royal Society's Copley Medal and the Presidential Medal of Freedom.

Did you know?
Hawking believes that time travel will be possible in future and humans will inhabit other planets.

How he changed the world

Stephen Hawking has experienced a meteoric rise to superstardom. His theories and writings now lead modern science, and they have expanded our understanding of the Universe.

British theoretical physicist **PAUL DIRAC** *did important work on quantum theory, which Hawking later worked on.*

British mathematician **ROGER PENROSE** *inspired Hawking by confirming that black holes develop from dying stars and introducing a theory of spacetime singularity, in 1965, to help understand gravity.*

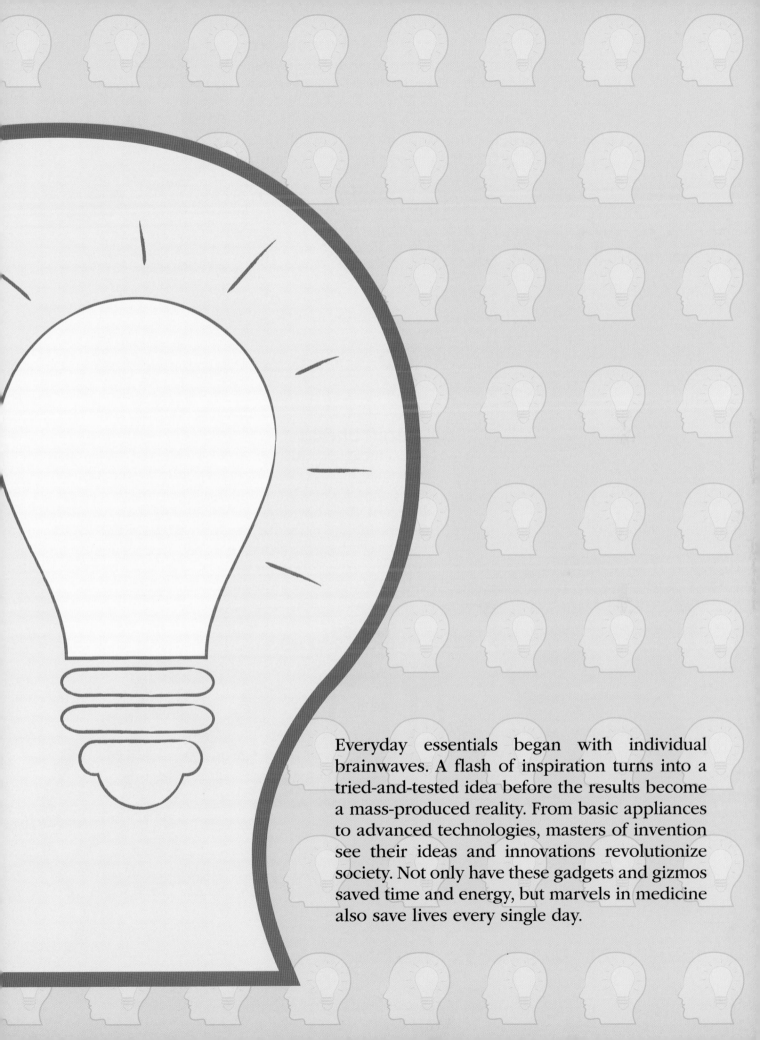

Everyday essentials began with individual brainwaves. A flash of inspiration turns into a tried-and-tested idea before the results become a mass-produced reality. From basic appliances to advanced technologies, masters of invention see their ideas and innovations revolutionize society. Not only have these gadgets and gizmos saved time and energy, but marvels in medicine also save lives every single day.

Set on steam

When James Watt was born in Scotland in 1736, **steam engines were slow, faulty, and dangerous**. Watt became interested in the power of steam. In 1758, a meeting about the *science of steam* with Joseph Black, a Scottish Chemist, inspired Watt to **RESEARCH STEAM POWER** and make his own equipment.

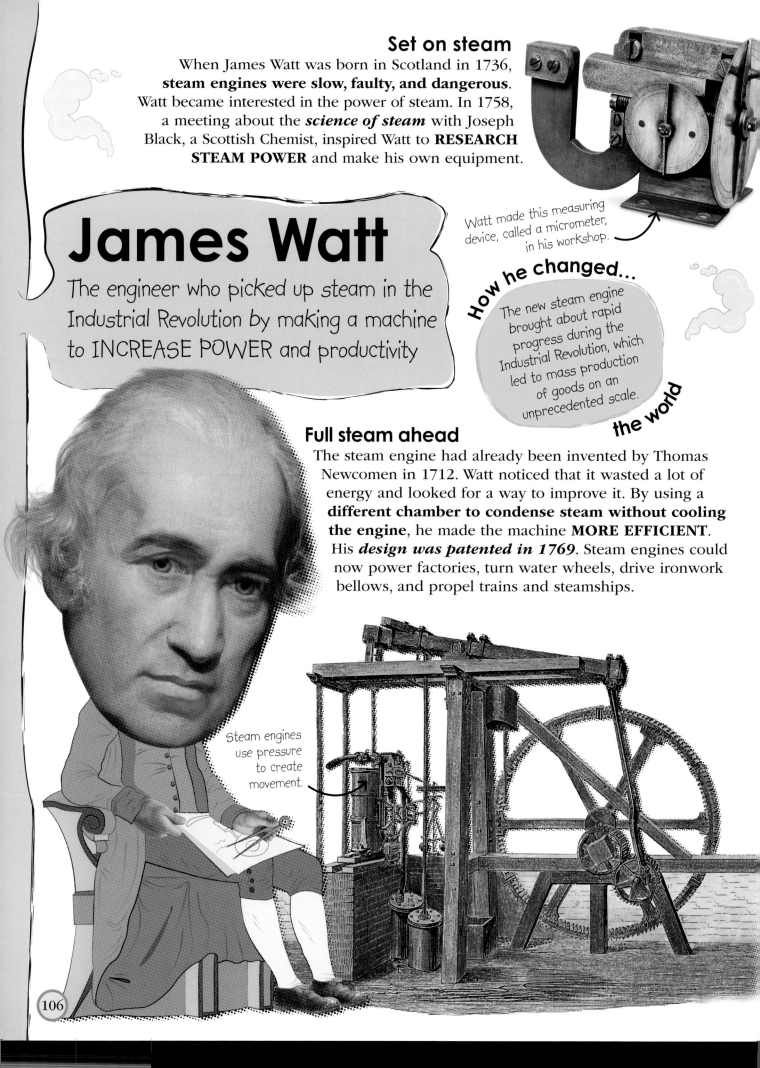

Watt made this measuring device, called a micrometer, in his workshop.

James Watt

The engineer who picked up steam in the Industrial Revolution by making a machine to INCREASE POWER and productivity

How he changed...

The new steam engine brought about rapid progress during the Industrial Revolution, which led to mass production of goods on an unprecedented scale.

the world

Full steam ahead

The steam engine had already been invented by Thomas Newcomen in 1712. Watt noticed that it wasted a lot of energy and looked for a way to improve it. By using a **different chamber to condense steam without cooling the engine**, he made the machine **MORE EFFICIENT**. His *design was patented in 1769*. Steam engines could now power factories, turn water wheels, drive ironwork bellows, and propel trains and steamships.

Steam engines use pressure to create movement.

Rudolf Diesel

The inventor in the hot seat with the
INTERNAL COMBUSTION ENGINE

Top student

Born in 1858 in Paris, France, Rudolf Diesel moved
to London with his family aged 12 to escape the
Franco-Prussian war. Graduating from the Technical
University of Munich in Germany with brilliant
results, he worked on various engineering projects,
including plans for a **refrigeration plant**. A lecture
about *thermodynamics* (the study of heat as a form
of energy) was a turning point, inspiring him to
design the **INTERNAL COMBUSTION ENGINE**.

Fuel injection valve
where the fuel enters

Diesel engine

Existing engines were big and slow, but Diesel
worked on a more **efficient design** in which
the fuel added to compressed air was ignited
by heat rather than a spark. In 1893, he
received his patent for the new internal
combustion engine. Named after the inventor, it
was called the **DIESEL ENGINE**. Running on
cheap fuel with twice the efficiency of steam
engines, the *diesel engine was a huge success*.

Compressed air heats up
inside the cylinders, and
the high temperature
ignites the fuel.

How he changed...

Factories, generators,
and the modern
transport system are all
powered by engines
based on Diesel's
original designs.

the world

Computing creatives

GENIUSES who revolutionized the world of computing

There aren't many areas of modern life that haven't been changed by computers. In the world of computer science, these gifted geeks were trailblazers.

Ada Lovelace

The daughter of poet Lord Byron, Ada Lovelace developed *a passion for mathematics* as a child. After meeting British mathematician Charles Babbage in 1833, she wrote detailed notes about his calculating machine, the Analytical Engine. She then created a set of instructions, or an **algorithm**, to make the machine perform different functions. By doing this, she became the world's **FIRST COMPUTER PROGRAMMER**.

Did you know
After a moth got trapped in a computer, Hopper coined the term "bug" for a computer glitch.

Grace Murray Hopper

American Grace Murray Hopper began working with computers when she joined the United States Navy in 1943. She believed that *programming should be accessible to all*, so she created FLOW-MATIC, the world's first programming language to use **ENGLISH WORDS** instead of mathematical symbols. This led to the development of COBOL, and laid the groundwork for languages such as **Scratch and Python**.

John von Neumann

In 1945, this Hungarian-American mathematician worked out a model for a **computer that could store programs**. All computers since then have been based on this model. The infrastructure, known as the **VON NEUMANN ARCHITECTURE**, was a breakthrough, allowing the use of memory to *store sequences of instructions as well as data*.

Annie Easley

Starting her career at the *National Advisory Committee for Aeronautics* (now NASA) in 1955, Annie Easley became one of the first African-American computer programmers. She was **instrumental** in **DEVELOPING SOFTWARE** for Centaur, a high-energy booster rocket that was used to launch satellites and spacecraft.

Tim Berners-Lee

The way we share information was changed forever when this British **computing whizz** launched the **WORLD WIDE WEB (WWW)** in 1991. This is the vast collection of linked websites made possible by the Internet. Berners-Lee also created the world's *first web browser*, a program that allows us to locate and view websites.

Wilhelm Röntgen

The prize-winning PROFESSOR whose accidental discovery of invisible rays gave the green light for X-rays

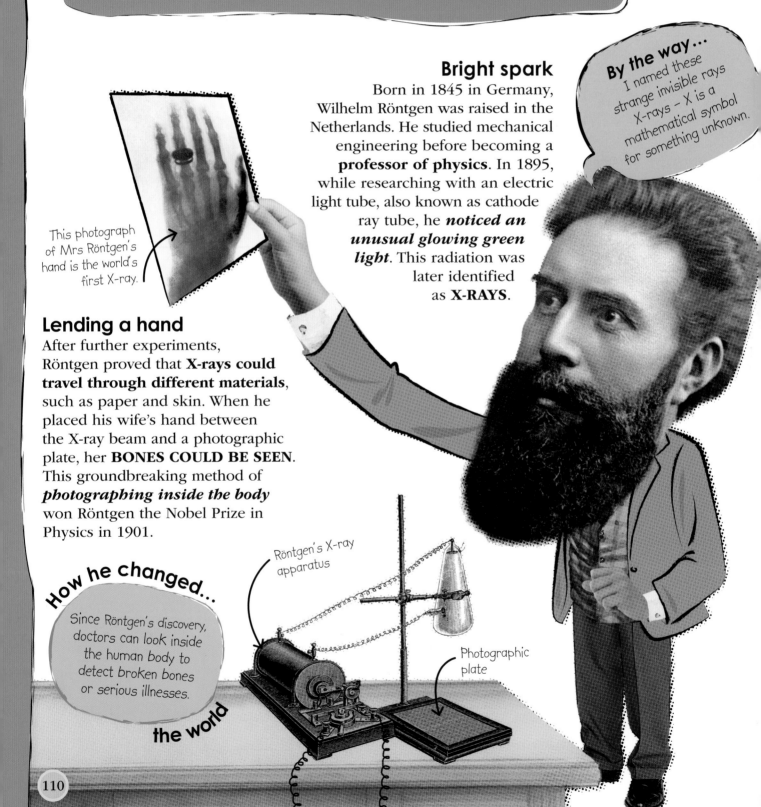

By the way...
I named these strange invisible rays X-rays – X is a mathematical symbol for something unknown.

Bright spark

Born in 1845 in Germany, Wilhelm Röntgen was raised in the Netherlands. He studied mechanical engineering before becoming a **professor of physics**. In 1895, while researching with an electric light tube, also known as cathode ray tube, he *noticed an unusual glowing green light*. This radiation was later identified as **X-RAYS**.

This photograph of Mrs Röntgen's hand is the world's first X-ray.

Lending a hand

After further experiments, Röntgen proved that **X-rays could travel through different materials**, such as paper and skin. When he placed his wife's hand between the X-ray beam and a photographic plate, her **BONES COULD BE SEEN**. This groundbreaking method of *photographing inside the body* won Röntgen the Nobel Prize in Physics in 1901.

How he changed...

Since Röntgen's discovery, doctors can look inside the human body to detect broken bones or serious illnesses.

Röntgen's X-ray apparatus

Photographic plate

the world

110

The blue sea

On an ocean voyage in 1921, Raman was struck by the intense **blue colour of the sea**. Rejecting the accepted view that the sea reflects the colour of the sky, he proposed the colour was a result of white **sunlight being scattered** (reflected in many directions) as it hit water molecules. When this happens, a part of the light changes colour to blue at it scatters. This was called **THE RAMAN EFFECT**. For this discovery, he won the Nobel Prize in Physics in 1930.

Raman used this pocket spectrometer to measure wavelengths of light.

Raman was born in Trichy, a city in southern India.

Early life

Chandrasekhara Venkata Raman was born in India in 1888. Raman was always fascinated by natural phenomena and began his **research into light and sound waves** while he was still a **STUDENT**. In 1917, he became a **Professor of Physics** at Calcutta University.

When light waves enter the water, some of the light reflects and some gets absorbed by the water.

How he changed...

The science behind the Raman Effect has many important applications today, from detecting diseases to identifying minerals.

the world

C V Raman

The Indian physicist who figured out why the SEA APPEARS BLUE

Nikola Tesla

Switched-on supplier of the ELECTRIC CURRENT

This electric eccentric created countless inventions that led to the global generation of power.

> **By the way...**
> I took risks with my experiments, even causing a building to vibrate so badly that people thought there had been an earthquake!

Visionary inventor

Born in 1856, Tesla *enjoyed watching his mother invent various domestic appliances* at home. After college, he took a job at the Central Telephone Exchange in Budapest, Hungary, in 1880. He said that seeing all the flashing lights sparked **VISIONS OF NEW INVENTIONS**. The first was a **machine that amplified the sound on a telephone**.

Tesla's induction motor used a rotating magnetic field to create movement.

Who came before...

The relationship between electromagnetic force and electric current was first established by French physicist **ANDRÉ-MARIE AMPÈRE** *in 1820.*

In 1822, British physicist **PETER BARLOW** *invented a basic electric machine called Barlow's wheel, which was the first device to be powered by electromagnetism.*

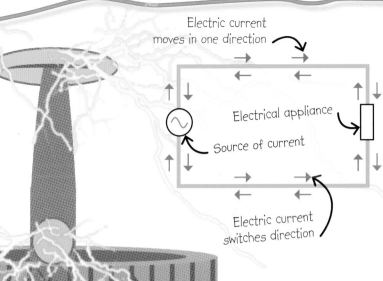

Electric current moves in one direction

Electrical appliance

Source of current

Electric current switches direction

Alternative power

Tesla moved to the USA in 1884 and started working on **alternating current** (AC). This was a **NEW ELECTRICAL SYSTEM** in which the flow of electricity around a circuit continually changes direction, in comparison to direct current (DC), which always flows in one direction. Tesla thought AC would *make it easier to transport electricity across long distances.*

Electric current from a Tesla Coil can be transmitted wirelessly.

AC inventions

In 1883, Tesla **invented the world's first induction motor**. This design ran on his new AC power, *using a rotating magnetic field to create movement*. He went on to develop the **TESLA COIL**, which produced AC power. He showcased his AC invention at the 1893 World Fair in Chicago.

How he changed the world

Nikola Tesla's electric motors keep the modern world running today, featuring in all kinds of everyday items and appliances.

The Tesla Coil was used in early wireless technology, such as radio transmitters.

Interior of Tesla's Niagara Falls power plant

Powering the planet

In 1895, Tesla's AC **hydroelectric power plant** was built at Niagara Falls. There was widespread media interest when the town of *Buffalo, New York, was powered using his new system*. The AC system would soon take over as the **WORLD'S LEADING POWER SOURCE**.

Did you know?
Nikola Tesla Day is celebrated across many parts of the USA on his birth date, 10 July.

American blacksmith **THOMAS DAVENPORT** *built the first American DC electric motor in 1834.*

German engineer **MORITZ VON JACOBI** *was the first to incorporate electromagnets in a motor design, which was used to propel a paddle boat across Russia's Neva River.*

Joseph Lister

The British surgeon who led the clean-up operation in 19th-century healthcare, setting new standards for hospital hygiene.

The founder of ANTISEPTIC medicine

Did you know?
Joseph Lister's father pioneered improved lenses for the compound microscope.

First public demonstration of the use of an anaesthetic in surgery

Surgical study

At the age of 19, Lister watched the **first public surgical procedure using anaesthetic** (medicine to stop someone feeling pain). Inspired by this, he studied **MEDICINE**, graduating in 1852. Later that year, he joined the Royal College of Surgeons and became a *surgeon* at the University College Hospital in London.

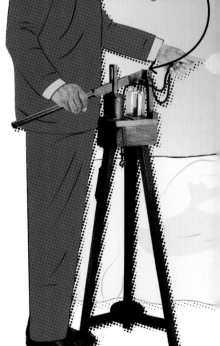

A "donkey engine", was used to spray phenol around the operating theatre.

Lister reveals germs on unwashed surgical instruments.

Pasteur's principles

Influenced by the work of French chemist Louis Pasteur, Lister **EXPERIMENTED** to confirm **that infections are caused by germs** and not bad air as was believed at the time. After noticing that almost half of amputation patients died from blood poisoning caused by germs, Lister was determined to *find a solution*.

Who came before...

JOHN HUNTER *was Britain's leading lecturer on surgery during the 18th century. At a time when most surgeons were not trained doctors, he advocated a scientific approach to surgical procedures.*

In the 19th century, Hungarian doctor **IGNAZ SEMMELWEIS** *was the first to observe a connection between hospital cleanliness and infection levels. He advised doctors to wash their hands thoroughly before operations to reduce infections.*

Antiseptic impact

Lister began using a chemical called **PHENOL**, also known as carbolic acid, to soak medical dressings. As a result, the death rate due to infection on Lister's ward plummeted and phenol became the **world's first antiseptic** (a chemical solution that kills germs). He also *introduced guidelines for hospital hygiene*, such as sterilizing medical instruments, and making sure everyone washed their hands frequently.

The use of antiseptics led to a rise in the number and complexity of surgeries.

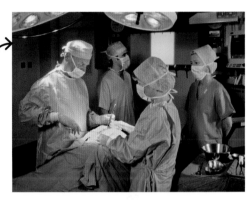

By the way...
Listerine mouthwash was named after me in 1879. It was originally used as an antiseptic before being sold as a cure for bad breath.

Awards and accolades

Lister was **WELL REWARDED** for his work. He became President of the Clinical Society of London and the Royal Society, as well as *recipient of the Royal Medal, Albert Medal, and Copley Medal*. Antiseptics have advanced a lot since Lister's death in 1912, and germ prevention continues to **make operations safer and more successful**.

How he changed the world

After Joseph Lister published his incredible findings, many countries adopted his healthcare techniques. As a result, infection rates dropped dramatically around the world.

Who came after...

Known as the Lady with the Lamp, British nurse **FLORENCE NIGHTINGALE** observed soldiers dying of infection because of unhygienic conditions in battlefield hospitals. She set about cleaning the rat-infested wards and improving efficiency in medical care.

During the 1890s, new measures were taken to improve hospital hygiene. American surgeon **WILLIAM STEWART HALSTED** introduced the wearing of rubber gloves during operations.

Alan Turing

The CODE-BREAKER who invented the computer age

Englishman Alan Turing not only helped to turn the tide of World War II, but also developed the idea of the modern computer.

Turing, aged 13, with his school friends

A maths genius

Alan Turing was a brilliant mathematician. In 1936, while still at the University of Cambridge, he outlined his theory of a **UNIVERSAL MACHINE**. This was **a device that could solve any problem** using a set of coded instructions that were stored in its memory – *an idea that paved the way for modern computer science*.

Cracking the code

During World War II, Turing joined the code-breakers working at *a top-secret British base, Bletchley Park*. The Germans were using a typewriter-like device called the **Enigma machine** to transmit coded military messages. Turing and his colleague Gordon Welchman developed the **BOMBE** machine to decode these messages. The machine played a crucial role in the victory of Allied forces over Germany.

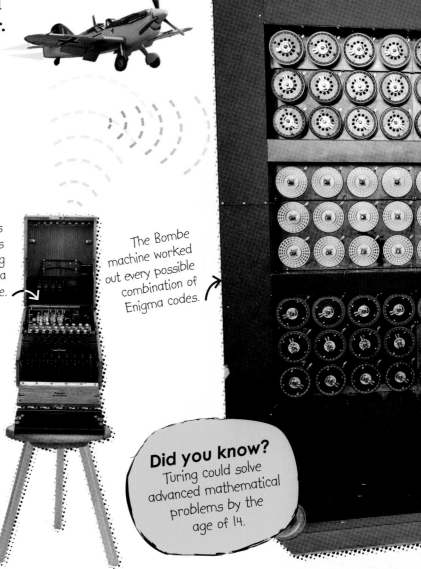

The Germans changed codes every day using the Enigma machine.

The Bombe machine worked out every possible combination of Enigma codes.

Did you know?
Turing could solve advanced mathematical problems by the age of 14.

What came before...

In the 1820s, English mathematician Charles Babbage designed and partially built a mechanical calculator called the **DIFFERENCE ENGINE**. *This device used arithmetical addition, and was powered by cranking a handle.*

American inventor Herman Hollerith built the first **TABULATING AND SORTING MACHINE** *in 1889. It used punched cards to record and process data; a clerk would sit at a desk and insert cards into the machine.*

The Pilot ACE was based on Turing's design.

This was the console for controlling the operations.

Onto computers

After the war, Turing *produced a design for a computer – the Automatic Computing Engine (ACE)*. Although it was never built, it led to the production of the world's first general-purpose computer called the **Pilot ACE** in 1950. Turing also researched whether a computer is a thinking machine, and created an experiment called the **TURING TEST** – a method to see whether a machine has human-like intelligence.

By the way...
I wrote the first ever chess computer program. I called it Turbochamp.

How he changed the world

Turing's code-breaking work shortened the war, saving millions of lives. His idea of an intelligent machine turned into a reality with the development of computers by the end of the 20th century.

What came after...

In 1958, American engineers Jack Kilby and Robert Noyce unveiled the **INTEGRATED CIRCUIT** – the first working microchip. Without this tiny device we would not have personal computers or mobile phones.

The first home computer, the **APPLE I**, was built by Americans Steve Wozniak and Steve Jobs in 1975. User-friendly and cheap, Apple computers revolutionized the home computer industry.

Alfred Nobel

The CHEMIST who blasted his way into history books

Nobel made his fortune by inventing dynamite and other powerful explosives, but his name is now associated with learning and peace.

Nobel as a young man

By the way... I named my explosive dynamite from the Greek word *dunamis*, which means power.

The young chemist

The son of a skilled engineer, Nobel was born in Stockholm, Sweden, in 1833. The family **moved to Russia in 1842**, where his father had *set up a firm making explosives and equipment* for the Russian navy. When Nobel was 17, he travelled abroad to study **CHEMISTRY**.

What came before...

Looking for a magic potion that would allow them to live forever, the ancient Chinese instead discovered the first chemical explosive – **GUNPOWDER**.

Molecular structure of nitroglycerine

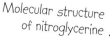

Italian chemist Ascanio Sobrero discovered the explosive **NITROGLYCERINE** *in 1847. However, he considered it too dangerous for practical use.*

Explosive discovery

In 1864, one of Nobel's brothers died in an explosion while working with liquid nitroglycerine – a very unstable explosive. Nobel became determined to find *a way of making nitroglycerine less dangerous*. By mixing it with a form of silica, he **developed a safer product** called **DYNAMITE**. It became widely used, not only in construction and mining, but also in warfare. Nobel's invention made him a wealthy man.

Those who are awarded the Nobel Prize receive a gold medal, which shows Nobel on the front.

The Nobel Prize

When Nobel died in 1896, his relatives were surprised to find out that he had left most of his vast fortune to fund *annual prizes for outstanding achievements in science, literature, and peace*. Since 1901, the **NOBEL PRIZE** has been **awarded every year on 10 December**, the anniversary of his death.

Dynamite transformed rock blasting, making it much easier to carry out work such as drilling tunnels.

How he changed the world

Dynamite revolutionized the construction and mining industries, and changed warfare. However, Nobel is best remembered for establishing the awards that encourage achievement.

What came after...

During the 1930s, dynamite was used as a blasting agent in huge engineering projects such as the **HOOVER DAM** in Nevada, USA.

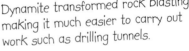

Since the 1950s, the explosive ammonium nitrate-fuel oil (**ANFO**) has largely replaced dynamite in the mining industry. ANFO detonates more slowly and is considered much safer than dynamite.

Guiding light

Javan was born in Tehran, the capital of Iran, but moved to the USA after World War II. He earned a PhD in physics from Columbia University in 1954. **Years of study and research** resulted in his invention of the world's first **GAS LASER** in 1960. This instrument carries an electric current through a gas to produce a strong light. Javan's gas laser was the *first laser to generate a constant beam of light*.

Ali Javan

The LEADING LIGHT whose invention shone across all areas of science

Javan's gas laser

Javan was awarded the Frederic Ives Medal in 1975.

How he changed...

An incredible feat of technology, the gas laser became a permanent feature in barcode scanners, medical equipment, and Internet data transmission.

the world

Hall of fame

Javan was a professor of physics at the Massachusetts Institute of Technology until the end of his career. He made *major breakthroughs* in different fields of physics, and established the USA's **FIRST RESEARCH BASE** for laser technology. A lifetime with lasers resulted in **many awards**, including entry in the National Inventors Hall of Fame in 2006.

Rachel Carson

A crusading CONSERVATIONIST who used the power of the written word to make the world a better place

How she changed...
the world

Carson's scientific writing about the dangers affecting nature on Earth encouraged future generations to embrace the environment and protect the planet.

Water writer

Born in 1907 in rural Pennsylvania, USA, Rachel Carson enjoyed being **surrounded by nature**. After gaining a master's degree in zoology, Carson worked as a **marine biologist** and then became the chief editor at the US Fish and Wildlife Service. This work motivated her to publish an award-winning **SCIENTIFIC STUDY of the sea**, called *The Sea Around Us* in 1951, which was translated into 28 languages.

Carson researched marine ecology, including seawater and seaweed.

Pesticide problem

Carson was worried about chemical pesticides, designed to protect crops by killing pests. Research revealed their **harmful chemicals** were destroying food chains and fragile ecosystems (networks of livings things found in an area). In 1962, Carson detailed these dangers in her book *Silent Spring*. Later, she called for new policies to **PROTECT** the environment. Although many people were sceptical of her ideas at first, she eventually convinced governments to use pesticides more responsibly.

A PENGUIN BOOK

Rachel Carson

'... what we have to face is not an occasional dose of poison which has accidentally got into some article of food, but a persistent and continuous poisoning of the whole human environment...'

Silent Spring

The title *Silent Spring* was inspired by the number of birds dying from eating food contaminated with chemical pesticides and the sad prospect of a springtime without birdsong.

Communicators

AMBASSADORS across all areas of science with voices instantly recognizable to millions

Scientific subjects are often complex ideas, but an engaging and enlightening spokesperson can make even the most difficult topics easier to understand.

> **Did you know?**
> At least 10 plants and animals have been named after David Attenborough.

David Attenborough

Veteran voice of the natural world, David Attenborough is one of **Britain's best-loved broadcasters**. A natural sciences graduate in 1947, he went on to write, produce, and host wildlife documentaries. First shown in 2006, the popular *Planet Earth* series showed high-definition footage of animals in their natural habitats, accompanied by Attenborough's **DISTINCTIVE** narration.

Carl Sagan

American astronomer Carl Sagan was excited by the Universe as a young boy. After studying astronomy and astrophysics at the University of Chicago, he became a professor, author, **advisor to NASA** (the USA's space agency), and television presenter, sharing his enthusiasm for space across various media. Televised in 1980, Sagan's series *Cosmos* was watched by many millions of viewers.

Dava Sobel

American science reporter Dava Sobel began **writing the real stories behind scientific subjects**. Her books include *The Glass Universe*, the story of women at Harvard Observatory, USA, studying the stars, and *A More Perfect Heaven*, the story of how Nicolaus Copernicus changed views about the Solar System and the cosmos. In 2001, the National Science Board **HONOURED** Sobel for *raising public awareness of science*.

Bill Nye

Best known for his 1990s show *Bill Nye, the Science Guy*, William Sanford Nye is an American science educator. This science and mathematics wizard **simplifies his vast knowledge** to help children understand difficult subjects. Nye also helped develop **SUNDIALS** for the Mars Rover missions. He is now serving as the head of The Planetary Society, an institute that promotes astronomy and space exploration.

Neil deGrasse Tyson

A trip to New York's Hayden Planetarium as a child ignited Neil deGrasse Tyson's interest in astronomy and, three decades later, he became that planetarium's **DIRECTOR**. Born in 1958, the American astrophysicist is **a gifted speaker on television, radio, and the Internet**. He uses *popular cultural references* to ensure his audience relates to scientific subject matter.

Let's applaud...

Discover the amazing achievements of these SCIENTIFIC SUPERSTARS from around the world.

Brahmagupta (598–670)

Indian astronomer Brahmagupta **wrote books on mathematics and astronomy** in poetry. He also **ESTABLISHED** rules for the *number zero, fractions, and positive and negative numbers*.

Bhāskara I (c.600–c.680)

The first person to **use a circle to represent zero** in the Hindu-Arabic numeral system was Indian **MATHEMATICIAN** and writer Bhāskara I. Although not much is known about his life, his writing centred on the *planets, stars, and eclipses of the Sun and Moon*.

Jane Marcet (1769–1858)

With the publication of her book *Conversations on Chemistry* in 1806, Englishwoman Jane Marcet became the world's **FIRST FEMALE SCIENCE WRITER**. Aimed at uneducated girls, her work soon **crossed the boundaries** of gender, age, and race.

When an electric current flows through a wire, it produces a magnetic field like a magnet.

André-Marie Ampère (1775–1836)

French physicist Ampère *established the new science* of electric currents and magnetic fields, now called electromagnetism. His name is still heard today with the term **AMPERE**, the **unit used to measure electric current**.

Johann Wolfgang Döbereiner (1780–1849)

German chemist Döbereiner was known for **spotting similarities between elements and grouping them together**. He **HELPED TO DEVELOP** *Dmitri Mendeleev's periodic table* into the version used today.

Mary Somerville (1780–1872)

The **existence of the planet Neptune** was correctly **PREDICTED** by this Scottish astronomer and science writer. In 1835, both Mary and German astronomer Caroline Herschel became the first female members of the *Royal Astronomical Society*.

Maria Mitchell (1818–1889)

This American astronomer is best known for *spotting a comet* through her telescope in 1847. At the time King Frederick VI of Denmark was giving prizes for the discovery of new comets, so **Miss Mitchell's Comet WON** her a medal.

George Washington Carver (c.1864–1943)

This African-American scientist and inventor was nicknamed the *Peanut Man* after his research on crops, including **peanuts, soybeans, and sweet potatoes**. He also developed the **TREATMENT** for polio patients using peanut oil for massages.

Linus Pauling (1901–1994)

With *hundreds of scientific papers* to his name, American chemist Pauling wrote about chemical bonds and biology. He was the **first person** to win two individual **NOBEL PRIZES** – for Chemistry in 1954 and for Peace in 1962.

Frederick Sanger (1918–2013)

Twice winner of the Nobel Prize in Chemistry, this British biochemist researched **INSULIN** and **DNA** to advance the areas of genetics and medicine. His **Sanger sequencing technique** (the method to determine the sequence of a DNA molecule) continues to be used today.

Katherine Johnson (born 1918)

This award-winning American mathematician worked as a **HUMAN COMPUTER** for NASA's predecessor – *National Advisory Committee for Aeronautics* (NACA). Johnson **worked out complex calculations for space missions**, including the trajectory for Alan Shepard, the first American in Space.

Jocelyn Bell Burnell (born 1943)

The **detection of radio pulses** in the sky during the 1960s was conducted by this Irish astrophysicist. She found they were *neutron stars* (the remains of a superweight star) emitting radio waves, now called **PULSARS**.

Masatoshi Shima (born 1943)

Japanese engineer Shima was the brains behind the design of the world's **FIRST MICROPROCESSOR** (the chip that controls a computer's function) – the Intel 4004. This **groundbreaking invention** was *manufactured in 1971*.

Shirley Ann Jackson (born 1946)

American physicist Shirley Ann Jackson laid the *foundations* for many future communication **DEVICES**, including fibre-optic cables and advanced additions to telephones and fax machines. **In 2014, she was awarded** the country's top prize, the National Medal of Science.

Craig Venter (born 1946)

The **HUMAN GENOME PROJECT**, which mapped human DNA, was masterminded by American biochemist Craig Venter. His institute also *created the genetic material of a bacterium* in 2010, resulting in the world's **first synthetic organism**.

Endeavour travelled 198 million Km (123 million miles) and circled Earth more than 4,600 times.

Mae C Jemison (born 1956)

History was made on 12 September 1992 when Jemison **BLASTED OFF** on board *Endeavour*, becoming the first African-American in Space. Since then, she has focused on **healthcare and technology** for developing nations.

Fabiola Gianotti (born 1960)

Italy's most prominent physicist is the first female **DIRECTOR-GENERAL** at CERN, the European Organization for Nuclear Research. Gianotti has **written more than 500 scientific articles** and has a *host of awards* to her name.

Brian Cox (born 1968)

This British professor of physics presents a wide **VARIETY OF SCIENCE PROGRAMMES**. A new generation of viewers can explore space, astronomy, and physics thanks to his **relaxed style** and *accessible commentary*.

Maryam Mirzakhani (1977–2017)

The first woman and Iranian to win the *biggest honour in mathematics*, the **FIELDS MEDAL**, was Maryam Mirzakhani. Her achievement in 2014 was the result of in-depth **study of geometric shapes and curved surfaces**.

Glossary

Alchemist
A person who studied an ancient form of science from which chemistry developed. Alchemists sought the philosopher's stone that turns metals such as lead or iron into gold.

Asteroid
A small rocky body orbiting the Sun. Most asteroids are in the Asteroid Belt, between Mars and Jupiter.

Atmosphere
The layer of gases that surrounds a planet.

Atom
The smallest part of an element that can exist. It consists of a nucleus of protons and neutrons, which is orbited by electrons.

Atomic bomb
A powerful bomb that causes an explosion by releasing the energy in atoms.

Atomic mass
The total number of protons and neutrons that an atom contains.

Cathode ray tube
A tube with a vacuum inside, in which cathode rays produce an image on a screen – used mainly in televisions and computer screens.

CFCs (chlorofluorocarbons)
Chemical compounds formed from chlorine, fluorine, and carbon. CFCs are believed to damage the ozone layer so their use is now restricted.

Chromosome
A thread-like structure in a cell's nucleus. Chromosomes are made of DNA and contain genes.

Compound
A substance that is formed from the atoms of two or more elements. Water is a compound of hydrogen and oxygen.

Diffraction
The deflection of waves as they pass small obstacles or go through narrow openings.

DNA (deoxyribonucleic acid)
The chemical inside chromosomes that lets parents pass genetic information on to their offspring.

Electron
A tiny particle with a negative electric charge that is found in the empty outer space around an atom's nucleus.

Element
A basic building block of matter made from identical atoms.

Fossil fuel
A fuel that has formed over millions of years from the remains of living things. Coal, oil, and gas are fossil fuels.

Gene
One of the instructions stored inside cells and required to build and operate an animal's body or a plant. Genes are passed on from parents to their offspring.

Gravity
A force of attraction between objects found throughout the Universe. The greater the object's mass, the greater its gravitational pull.

Microchip
A miniature circuit made from thousands or millions of separate electronic components.

Neutron
A particle with no electric charge in the nucleus of an atom.

Nuclear energy
A type of energy released in one of two ways – by joining atoms together to make a larger atom (fusion), or by splitting an atom (fission).

Nucleus
The central part of an atom made from protons and neutrons.

Organism
A living thing consisting of one or more cells.

Palaeontologist
A scientist who studies life forms that existed in former geological periods.

Patent
A government licence that gives the person or company the right of ownership for an invention.

Pesticide
A chemical used to destroy pests that cause damage to crops and plants.

Proton
A particle with a positive electric charge in the nucleus of an atom.

Radioactivity
The disintegration of the nuclei in an atom, causing radiation to be given off.

Seismologist
A scientist who studies earthquakes.

Spacetime
Physicists think that time and space are really closely related. They imagine a combination of space and time called spacetime.

Ultraviolet
A type of electromagnetic radiation with a wavelength shorter than visible light.

X-ray
A type of electromagnetic radiation with a wavelength shorter than ultraviolet radiation.

Zoology
A branch of biology that specializes in the study of animals.

Index

Acknowledgments

DK WOULD LIKE TO THANK:

Carron Brown for proofreading and the index; Mansi Agrawal, Sunita Gahir, and Neetika Malik Jhingan for design assistance; Smita Mathur, Suefa Lee, and Bharti Bedi for editorial assistance; and Ashok Kumar for colour assistance.